United States Army Combat Developments Command, Report of the Field Manual Review Board Annex B, Evolution of the United States Army Field Manual: Valley Forge to Vietnam, Part 1

Combat Operations Research Group (CORG), Virgil Ney

The BiblioGov Project is an effort to expand awareness of the public documents and records of the U.S. Government via print publications. In broadening the public understanding of government and its work, an enlightened democracy can grow and prosper. Ranging from historic Congressional Bills to the most recent Budget of the United States Government, the BiblioGov Project spans a wealth of government information. These works are now made available through an environmentally friendly, print-on-demand basis, using only what is necessary to meet the required demands of an interested public. We invite you to learn of the records of the U.S. Government, heightening the knowledge and debate that can lead from such publications.

Included are the following Collections:

Budget of The United States Government
Presidential Documents
United States Code
Education Reports from ERIC
GAO Reports
History of Bills
House Rules and Manual
Public and Private Laws

Code of Federal Regulations
Congressional Documents
Economic Indicators
Federal Register
Government Manuals
House Journal
Privacy act Issuances
Statutes at Large

UNITED STATES ARMY
COMBAT DEVELOPMENTS COMMAND

REPORT OF THE FIELD MANUAL REVIEW BOARD

Annex B

Evolution Of The United States Army Field Manual: Valley Forge To Vietnam

USACDC Action Control Number 10544

December 1966

STATEMENT #2 UNCLASSIFIED

DDC

SEP 27 1967

A

Form 14

FIELD MANUAL REVIEW BOARD
HEADQUARTERS, US ARMY COMBAT DEVELOPMENTS COMMAND
FORT BELVOIR, VIRGINIA

(14) CORG—M-244

(6) REPORT OF THE FIELD MANUAL REVIEW BOARD.

ANNEX B.

EVOLUTION OF THE UNITED STATES FIELD MANUAL
VALLEY FORGE TO VIETNAM.

(9) Memorandum rept.,

--

(10) Virgil Ney

(11) December 1966

(12) 176p

(15) DA-04-200—AMC-1623X

(16) CORG-13428

(089325)

U
173
.A2
Copy 2

COMBAT OPERATIONS
RESEARCH GROUP

CORG MEMORANDUM

CORG-M-244

EVOLUTION OF THE
UNITED STATES ARMY
FIELD MANUAL

Valley Forge
to Vietnam

by

Virgil Ney

January 1966

Prepared by
TECHNICAL OPERATIONS, INCORPORATED
COMBAT OPERATIONS RESEARCH GROUP
under
DA CONTRACT NO. DA-19-020-AMC-00525X
and
DA CONTRACT NO. DA-04-200-AMC-1623X
CORG Project No. 13428
for
HEADQUARTERS
UNITED STATES ARMY COMBAT DEVELOPMENTS COMMAND
FORT BELVOIR, VIRGINIA

BAR

ABSTRACT

The modern military text, or field
manual, has evolved over a period of
several hundred years. Historically,
military training literature traces its
beginnings to the writings of the ancient
Chinese, Greeks, and Romans. Until
the invention of printing and the advent
of general literacy, military instruction
was usually oral and not written. In the
United States Army, the evolution of the
field manual falls into two distinct periods: the American Revolution to World
War I, and World War I to 1966.

BARON VON STEUBEN
1730 - 1794

Photo Courtesy
National Park Service

CONTENTS

CONTENTS (Concluded)

LIST OF ILLUSTRATIONS

EVOLUTION OF THE
UNITED STATES ARMY FIELD MANUAL
Valley Forge to Vietnam

INTRODUCTION

This study covers generally the subject of the evolution of the field manual in the United States Army from Valley Forge to the present era. Considerable attention is given to the historical background of military literature. Historically, in the United States, the evolution of the field manual was dependent, for many years, upon the writings and publications of private individuals. The advent of the military educational system, that is, the Military Academy, The War College, The Command and General Staff College, and the Schools of the Arms and Services, standardized the materials to be included in the various manuals.

Specific mention is made of individuals who were instrumental in the evolution of the field manual in the United States Army. The most prominent was Major General Frederick William von Steuben, Inspector General of the United States Army at Valley Forge, where in 1778 he wrote the first manual for the Army. Others of significance to this field mentioned are Winfield Scott, Dennis Hart Mahan, Henry Wager Halleck, William J. Hardee, Silas Casey, James C. Duane, Emory Upton, George B. McClellan, Arthur L. Wagner, John F. Morrison, James A. Moss, Lesley J. McNair, and Sterling A. Wood.

Part I includes an Historical Background and continues from the American Revolution to World War I. There is a general discussion of the subject of military training literature from ancient times to the American Revolution. The growth and development of United States Army training literature is treated specifically during the period from the American Revolution up to and including World War I. Authors and their manuals are listed and discussed in some detail. The War Department, the Government Printing Office, and private, commercial publishers are noted in their relation to the production of military training manuals. The background development of the field Service Regulations, as the first modern field manual, is mentioned. The private manual publication program of individual army officers and commercial firms during World War I is dealt with in detail.

Part II covers the period from the end of World War I to the present day. Included is the period of the 1920's with the inauguration of a post-World War I

CORG-M-244

training literature program. The development of the Basic Field Manual
by the War Department in 1930, as a consolidation of the Training Regulations, is shown as the beginning of the modern system of field manuals.
The important contributions of the Schools of the Combat Arms and Technical Services to the training literature of World War II are noted. Headquarters, The Army Ground Forces and the Replacement and School
Command are shown as critical agencies in the establishment of requirements for, and production of, field manuals of World War II. The postwar reorganization and the replacement of Headquarters, Army Ground
Forces and the Replacement and School Command by Army Field Forces,
and eventually the Continental Army Command, is shown. The effects of
these changes are noted in relation to the training literature program of
the postwar Army.

The organization of the United States Army Combat Developments
Command in 1962 and its relationship to the initiation, revision, and
production of doctrinal field manuals is covered in detail.

The Korean War and its stimulation of the training literature program
of the United States Army is noted in some detail. The effect of Korea upon
the type of manual desired by the users, the troops, is covered.

The impact of the post-Korean period; the role of the Continental Army
Command; the establishment of the Combat Developments Command; are
discussed in light of doctrinal and applicatory field manual writing and
production. The impact of Vietnam upon the training literature program
is noted.

The appendixes contain materials of interest to the student of the
evolution of the United States Army field manual.

The Bibliography lists books, articles, and official and semiofficial
publications used or noted in the preparation of the study.

PART I

HISTORICAL BACKGROUND

... if the profession of us soldiers is not usually
included among the "learned professions", there is
yet enough in it for a man to spend a lifetime learning.
We do not claim to belong to a learned profession in
any sense which makes it our object to study books
rather than men. No books will ever make a man a
soldier. No books will do him any service which tend
to distract his thoughts from the study of men, from
the care and command of men, from sympathy with
men, from learning to deal with men, from active life,
from practical energy. No books will supply the place
of instinctive genius for war. (Colonel Sir Frederick
Maurice, emphasis added)

2

Printed books for use in the instruction of military personnel in the theory and practice of their duties originated in the western world in the 15th century. The invention of the printing press by Guttenburg of Mainz, Germany gave rise to the printing trade. After the sacking of Mainz in 1462, the German printers fled and settled in Venice, Florence, Paris, Basle, Antwerp, and London. A number of books on the military art were printed at those places. The ancient military classics by such authors as Vegetius, Valtur, Cataneo, and Machiavelli were revived and published. The latter's Art of War was especially popular.

Aside from the interest in the revival of the authors of antiquity, the preoccupation of society with the subject of war caused much demand for these works. As war was a part-time occupation of the noble or gentleman of that day, and these groups were usually literate, the military books found their way into their hands. The rank and file, the peasant conscript or the professional member of a mercenary company, was generally illiterate and the printed word was of little interest or use to him.

The classical studies of war, as reissued by the early printers and publishers, were essentially works covering organization, formations, order of battle, and tactics. Personal knowledge of these subjects was considered necessary for the conduct of war by the gentleman warrior of the times. The art of war had not as yet become, in reality, a profession. True, there were professional mercenaries and companies of hired soldiers such as the condottieri[1] but most of the warriors were amateurs. Generally, military instruction during this period of history was by personal tutor. Those who conducted military instruction were often officers and former officers who had "returned from the wars" and were able to pass on their combat experiences to their students. The professional officer and soldier did not appear upon the scene until several hundred years later. The officer corps of Frederick the Great of Prussia came close to constituting a professional military group. Those who had been in campaigns under successful commanders sometimes hired themselves out to foreign sovereigns and nations as military advisors and instructors. As yet, there was no organized military profession. There were no formal schools of military instruction comparable to the Cadettenschule of Frederick the Great. In the cadet school of Frederick, the sons of the Junkers, or minor nobles, were trained from boyhood in the Prussian profession of arms.

In China in 500 B. C. (two thousand years before the European treatises) Sun Tsu Wu, a military philosopher and scholar, was writing his classic,

---

[1] A name given in the 14th century to the leaders of certain bands of military adventurers in Italy who, for booty, offered their services to any contest, and often practiced warfare on their own account purely for the sake of plunder. The Compagnies Grandes in France at about the same period were somewhat similar to the condottieri, and were so powerful at one time that in 1361 they routed the king's forces at Brignais and slew Jacques de Bourbon, constable of France. (Wilhelm's Gazetteer)

The Art of War. Because of its early date, Sun Tsu's work is considered the oldest military treatise in the world. Translated centuries later by renowned scholars, Sun Tsu's book was the first to lay down definite principles for the conduct of war. Above and beyond this achievement, the Art of War contributed much basic theory to the military art. This was especially noted in the fields of organization, unit control, and tactics. In essence, the great Chinese scholar's work was not a field manual, yet in the manner of a field manual. it established doctrine for field commanders (Ref 1).

At the time of the writings of Sun Tsu, the profession of arms had not been recognized as a full-time occupation. Oriental armies were in reality huge masses of illiterate peasant conscripts officered by the nobles. In general, the trade of the soldier was held in low esteem by Chinese society. The often-repeated saying "One does not make nails of good iron", meant that, in China, one did not use good men for soldiers. On the scale of Chinese society at that period of Chinese history, and in contemporary times, the soldier was found at the bottom. The writings in the field of war and the techniques of warfare were considered to be intellectual exercises within the realm of the scholar and philosopher. The management of an army was an essential part of the administrative and political skill of the emperor. As he did not often command in the field, he needed individuals who were qualified as generals to perform this duty for him. It was with this in mind that Sun Tsu promulgated his philosophy of war in his immortal Art of War.

Machiavelli, in his book The Prince, established principles and doctrine of war and peace for governing the actions of a ruler of a state. This volume has been extensively quoted since its publication. Summarizing the art of war and peace, the book has come to be regarded over the centuries as a manual for dictators and authoritarian rulers. Its connection with The Art of War is coincidental as having been written by the same author. However, the Art of War must be considered as one of the important early Western writings on the art of war. Written from both a doctrinal and technical point of view, the work qualifies as a manual (Refs 2 and 3).

The American College Dictionary defines a manual as follows: "a small book, esp. one giving information or instructions". In the Western World the idea of a manual, from the Latin manus, connoted a "handbook" or "pocketbook". The size of the book was governed to a great extent by the portability expected of the work. For the soldier, in the field or in the camp, the manuals were necessarily small and compact because of the limitation of space and materials. The manual thus became noted for containing a great amount of information in a small and limited number of printed pages. In all armies, manuals were often supplied with illustrations and diagrams.

Western society and its military community drew initially upon the historical experiences of the Greeks and the Romans for basic tactics and techniques of war. Before the advent of gunpowder, warfare was largely

4

a matter of organized and personally directed mass hand-to-hand combat. When available, instructional material consisted principally of lessons and plans for tactics, drilling, and marching. The order of battle was a most important item of instruction for senior and general officers. The technique of how to form units for battle was reduced to a series of printed tables which were published by Cataneo in London in 1588. This latter publication was, of course, in the era of gunpowder when war had become less muscular and direct by virtue of the propellant power of a proper mixture of charcoal and saltpeter (Ref 4).

De Re Militari, written by the Roman, Flavius Vegetius Renatus, was an attempt to collect and analyse the ancient writings, especially the military manuscripts, which contained the regulations and military customs of the Roman Legions. This work by Vegetius was destined to become the "military bible" for European soldiers and to survive as such well into the nineteenth century. Oddly, the preceptive writings of Vegetius were not heeded by the Romans for whom the manuscript was, in fact, written. There were several reasons for this lack of interest in this basic field manual of antiquity, among them:

> The decay of the Roman armies had progressed too
> far to be arrested by Vegetius' plea for a return to the
> virtues of discipline and courage of the ancients. At the
> same time, Vegetius' hope for a revival of the ancient
> organization of the legion was impracticable. Cavalry
> had adopted the armor of the foot soldier and was just
> commencing to become the principal arm of the military
> forces. The heavy-armed foot soldier, formerly the back-
> bone of the legion, was falling a victim to his own weight
> and relative immobility, and the light-armed infantry,
> unable to resist the shock of cavalry, was turning more
> to missile weapons. By one of the strange mutations of
> history, when later the cross-bow and gunpowder deprived
> cavalry of its shock power, the tactics of Vegetius again
> became ideal for armies, as they had been in the times
> from which he drew his inspiration (Ref 5, pp 2 and 3).

De Re Militari (Of Military Matters), or as translated, the Military Institutions of the Romans, was actually written as five books, three of which were translated by Lieutenant Clark of the British Army in 1767. The three books are titled respectively: Book I, Selection and Training of New Levies; Book II, Organization of the Legion; Book III, Dispositions For Action. There is little known about Vegetius. He was obviously a scholar and observer of the Roman scene but his military experience was not extensive. His function was really that of a military historian who based his writings and findings upon the writings of renowned Roman military leaders and rulers. Among these were Cato The Elder, Cornelius Celsus, Patermus, and Frontinus. The regulations of the Emperors such as Augustus, Trajan, and Hadrian formed the basic pattern of his classic military work.

The military experiences of the ancients were used to form the patterns of the early instructional manuals and discourses upon the military art. The ancient Greek and Roman classicists and commentators as Herodotus, Homer, Thucydides, Xenophon, Socrates, Onasander, Caesar, and Vegetius were found to be the most useful for the military planner and soldier of the 14th and 15th centuries. There were several reasons for the validity of these ancient works as guides for military training and operations. The primary reason was that they were based upon principles which had stood the test of battle and the passage of time.

> As far back in Greek literature as we may go, we find mention of military study, and of the professional military instructor. Socrates, himself a practical soldier, whose whole war service was in the ranks, so far appreciated the value of this instruction as to advise pupils who had military aspirations to avail themselves of it - reserving to himself, however, full liberty to inquire into the nature of the instruction given, and to criticize it (Ref 6, p 14).

Another cogent reason, historically, was that victory or defeat resulted from certain actions taken or ordered by the leaders. Until the discovery of gunpowder and its employment to propel missiles in warfare, battles were mass physical combats. Maneuvers on the battle field were principally those of mass movement of men and animals in order to effect proper contact for the initiation of the physical struggle. Military instruction during this period of history consisted primarily of basic weapon training and foot drill, as a member of the phalanx or the legion formation. For centuries after the discovery of gun powder, military science continued along the same pattern. The drill of the parade ground or barrack square was carried over to the field of combat. There was no special formation or drill for fighting and soldiers were commanded in battle as though they were automatons. Until cavalry appeared there was little attention paid to tactics and mobility. So, in essence, until after the American Civil War of 1861-1865 there was little attention given to the tactical movement of small units upon the field of battle (Ref 7).

In the beginning of the American Revolution, the American troops followed the English system of tactics as prescribed for the British Service. The advent of Baron von Steuben's "Blue Book" and its adoption by Congress in 1779 as the regulation for the Army of The United States gave the Americans a tactical system which differed from that of the English. Although based primarily upon the experience of von Steuben in the Prussian military establishment, the new drill regulations were adapted by the author to the American soldier.

Von Steuben's little volume continued as the official regulation of the fledgling United States Army until the War of 1812. The militia of the various states continued to reprint the "Blue Book" until the late 1830's (Ref 8).

> Perhaps no foreigner had ever done more to make Americans set a high value on military art and to show

how it could serve our particular system to best advantage. Von Steuben accomplished this difficult feat at a time when efforts for liberty were ebbing very low. To the ultimate triumph we must assign him no small measure of credit and devotion. Americans were aware that valor alone is never sufficient. Training, painstaking and complete, will be forever requisite, and this above all is what Steuben admirably contributed to the formative years of the Republic (Ref 9, p 10).

In 1812, General Alexander Smyth of the United States Army brought out a version of the French tactical regulations of 1791. This volume was actually published with the approval of the War Department and was not much more than an abridgment of Reglement Concerant l'Exercise et les Manoeuvres de l'Infanterie; du ler Aout, 1791. Thus the French influence within the American military was added to the tempered Prussian version already established by the devoted example and published writings of von Steuben.

The paucity of materials on the subject of regulations, tactics, and military administration impaired alike the discipline and efficiency of the army, and formed an almost insurmountable barrier to the progress of the officer ambitious to excel in, or even attain a fair knowledge of, the theoretical part of his profession. This fact was forcibly presented to the War Department by Captain Winfield Scott, of the new light artillery regiment, in a letter dated July 14, 1809, in which he requested to be sent to Europe to collect and compile materials for supplying the army with treatises on military police, discipline, and tactics. Referring to the limited knowledge of officers regarding the proper management and uses of horse artillery, the writer remarked: "The recent introduction of this important corps into the American service, and its peculiar duties and organization, leave it certain that it can be but imperfectly practiced or understood in this country. France is the best school for obtaining a knowledge of it". Captain Scott's proposition was not accepted. It was left for him, six years later, when, as a general officer of the regular army, he visited Europe, to collect the necessary data for the first comprehensive system of regulations given to the regular army, and which, to use General Scott's words, after being "obscured, mutilated, and pirated from 1836 down to 1861, inclusive" forms the foundation on which rest the army regulations of the present day (Ref 10, p 301).

During the war, in 1813, Lieutenant Colonel William Duane of the rifle regiment, prepared and published a handbook entitled Regulations to be Received and Observed For the Discipline of Infantry in The Army of the United States. The Secretary of War directed by General Order..."The Handbook For Infantry compiled and published by...will be received and observed as the system of Infantry Discipline for the Army of the United States." In connection with Colonel Duane's "Hand Book", it should be noted that he had published a Military Library which possessed considerable value as a repository of professional military information (Ref 11).

In presenting his volume to the public, Lieutenant Colonel William Duane showed the spirit of the times three years before the war of 1812:

> There is no discipline; there is seen no system; and there are gross misconceptions on the subject. There appears to have been a disposition to discourage the acquisition of military knowledge (Ref 11, p 144).

His work consisted of seven parts, touching on almost every phase of contemporary military education. But it was complicated and the natural result of the state of the times he shows above.

> At the outbreak of the War of 1812, the French system, as interpreted by Colonel Alexander Smyth and Lt. Colonel William Duane, gained the upper hand and was officially codified in 1815 by a board of officers under General Winfield Scott. This work, known familiarly thereafter as "Scott's Exercise", supplanted von Steuben in the regular army. Later, various "Compends" of the work were published for use by volunteers and militia, several by one Paraclete Potter of Poughkeepsie, N.Y., whose first name efficiently implies sufficient divine revelation to make his works preferred above all others (Ref 12, pp iii and iv).

Because of the wartime situation in 1813, Congress requested the President to have prepared and submitted to it for approval "a military system of discipline for the Infantry of the Army and Militia of the United States." But on account of the occupation of the Army with the almost disastrous campaigns in the field, the request of the Congress was not acted upon. Hence, it should be noted that during the period of the War of 1812, insofar as tactical instruction of the troops was concerned, every officer was a law unto himself (Ref 13, pp 137 and 138).

Winfield Scott, a young brigadier general of the United States Army instructed his troops at the camp near Buffalo, New York from a poor English translation published in Boston and an original copy of the French Tactics. Using these makeshift training manuals, General Scott trained two brigades of Major General Brown's division. How well they were trained may be judged by the British exclamation, upon seeing them advancing, "Those are Regulars, by God!" The exclusive and historical introduction of the French tactical system into the United States Army

CORG-M-244

was first noted at this camp of instruction under the command of General Scott. The French drill and tactical instruction, slightly modified, were adopted by the War Department and known throughout the regular service as "the system of 1815". By 1820, the system of 1815 was ordered adopted by the militia (Ref 15, p 135).

In 1825, a Board of Officers, headed by Major General Winfield Scott, promulgated the "System of 1825" which was a conglomeration of Prussian, French, French Revolutionary, and Napoleonic drill regulations and tactics. Adopted by the War Department, the System of 1825 remained as a standard for the United States Army until 1834. At this time, General Scott was authorized to adapt the Prussian system of drill and tactics to the American scene. This work was to carry Scott's name and was known generally throughout the military service as "Scott's Tactics". This useful work was to survive until the translations and adaptations of the French drill manual by Lieutenant Colonel William J. Hardee of the United States Army. Hardee's Tactics covered all units up to and including the battalion. Brigadier General Silas Casey of the United States Army revised Hardee during the Civil War (Colonel Hardee went South and became a Confederate Lieutenant General). General Casey added chapters covering the tactics of the Division and Corps d'Armee to his authorized version of Hardee (Ref 14).

THE AMERICAN REVOLUTION

> We believe that Baron von Steuben has made us soldiers, and that he is capable of forming the whole world into a solid column and deploying it from the center. We believe in his Blue Book. We believe in General Knox and his artillery. And we believe in our bayonets. (In the "Creed" of the American officers adopted at Verplanck's Point in 1782.)

The military instructional manuals available to the American Revolutionary Army were by custom and availability usually British in origin. There were, of course, some from the French service and a very limited few from the Germany of Frederick the Great. The following comment of A. S. K. Brown, President of The Company of Military Historians, in the introduction to the reprint of Nesmith's Soldier's Manual is significant:

> At the outbreak of our Revolutionary War, various European texts had been hastily reprinted to guide the continental soldier; but it was not until after General Baron von Steuben's regulations for the Order and Discipline of the Troops of the United States, based on the Prussian system, was approved by Washington and published in Philadelphia in 1779, that any one became official (Ref 12, p iii).

An example of the reprinting of a British manual is found in the publication of Military Instruction For Officers Detached in the Field;

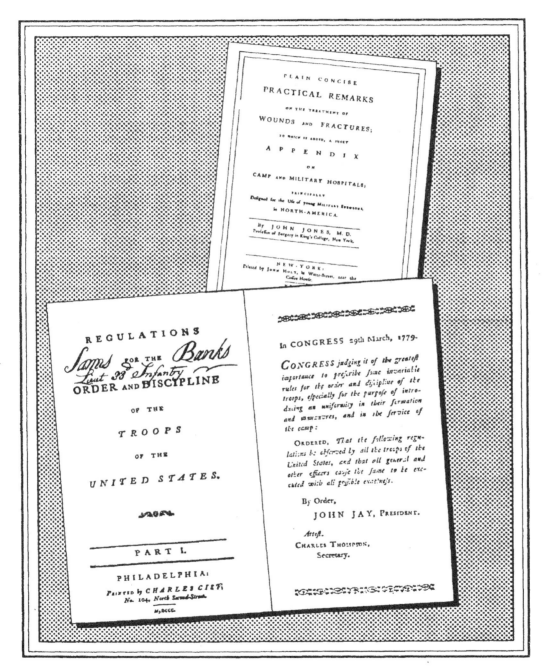

PLAIN CONCISE
PRACTICAL REMARKS
ON THE TREATMENT OF
WOUNDS AND FRACTURES;
TO WHICH IS ADDED, A SHORT
APPENDIX
ON
CAMP AND MILITARY HOSPITALS;
PRINCIPALLY
Designed for the Use of young MILITARY SURGEONS,
in NORTH-AMERICA.

By JOHN JONES, M.D.
Professor of Surgery in King's College, New York.

NEW-YORK:
Printed by JOHN HOLT, in Water-Street, near the
Coffee House.

REGULATIONS
Sams FOR THE *Banks*
Lieut 33 Infantry
ORDER AND DISCIPLINE
OF THE
TROOPS
OF THE
UNITED STATES.

PART I.

PHILADELPHIA:
Printed by CHARLES CIST,
No. 104, North Second-Street.
M,DCCC.

In CONGRESS 29th March, 1779.

CONGRESS judging it of the greatest
importance to prescribe some invariable
rules for the order and discipline of the
troops, especially for the purpose of intro-
ducing an uniformity in their formation
and manœuvres, and in the service of
the camp:

ORDERED, That the following regulations be observed by all the troops of the
United States, and that all general and
other officers cause the same to be exe-
cuted with all possible exactness.

By Order,

JOHN JAY, PRESIDENT.

Attest,
CHARLES THOMPSON,
Secretary.

Containing A Scheme For Forming A Corps of A Partisan by Roger Stevenson, Esquire, Philadelphia; 1775. Examples of the British manuals produced in England but available in the Colonies were A Treatise of Military Discipline published in London in 1746 by Major General Humphrey Bland of the British Army; Military Guide For Young Officers by Thomas Sime, originally published in London but reprinted in Philadelphia in 1776. Essai sur l'art de la guerre published in Paris by Lancelot, Turpin de Crisse in 1754 and translated into English by Captain Joseph Otway of the British Army in London in 1761.

Friedrich Wilhelm Ludolf Gerhard Augustin, Baron von Steuben (1730-1794), Major General and Inspector General of The United States Army at Valley Forge, was the father of the field manual of The United States Army. Coming to America as a volunteer at her darkest hour while her Army was starving and freezing at the winter encampment at Valley Forge, Pennsylvania, this former member of the staff of Frederick the Great, breathed new military life into the disorganized and dispirited body of American patriots.

> Training was making little progress, for there was neither interest nor uniformity of method. Each commanding officer gave such instruction as he would or could, selecting material from some one of the few drill manuals available (Ref 15, p 87).

Training and discipline were needed badly and von Steuben supplied them both. His methods were often unusual and unorthodox but they were effective. His first step in the revitalization of the Continental Army was most significant of things to come.

> He began operations by drafting 120 men from the line, forming them into a guard for the general-in-chief. He made this guard his military school. He drilled it twice a day and, to remove the English and American prejudice that to drill recruits was a sergeant's duty beneath the station of an officer, he took a musket and showed the men the manual exercises.

> His example was contagious, and Valley Forge became a great training camp, where the American officers, for the first time in history, became the instructors of their men. He appointed inspectors for each division, and all of his inspectors were present at each drill. In two weeks, his company knew how to bear arms, had a military air, knew how to march, to form column, deploy, and execute small maneuvers and exercises.

> Von Steuben had a free hand in regard to the men in his company. They were well dressed, their arms were clean and in good order, and their general appearance was quite respectable. He paraded them in the

presence of all the officers of the Army and gave them an opportunity to exhibit what they knew. They formed in column, deployed, attacked with the bayonet, changed front, etc. The company formed a new and agreeable sight for the young officers and soldiers. Having demonstrated his method of drill, von Steuben dispersed his apostles, the inspectors, and his new doctrines were largely embraced. He lost no time in extending his operations upon a large scale. He applied his system to battalions, to brigades, and in a short time, he maneuvered an entire division in the presence of the commander-in-chief (Ref 16, pp 291 and 292).

A number of the officers who reported to General George Washington at Cambridge were practical soldiers, if not professionals. Two, Horatio Gates and Charles Lee, had seen service under the King's commission. Hence, the military education and background presumably fitted them for high command in the Continental Line. Oddly, both did not fare too well in the command of the "rabble in arms". Others who had served in the French and Indian War rose to high and important commands during their service. Perhaps their degrees of skill in arms may be ascribed to the following reasons, as shown in the extract from Jacobs, The Beginning of the U.S. Army:

When they returned home they sought opportunity to supplement this knowledge by studying British books on military art. These were easy to obtain and widely read. Washington had some of the best in his own library. Henry Knox sold a number of them in his book store at Boston. The Norfolk Militia Discipline, or a modification of it, was popular in the northern colonies. It had been published in England after the passage of the Militia Bill of 1757. Another was the British Manual of 1764, commonly known as the "Sixty-fourth". In the South, Colonel Bland's treatise had been in vogue for years. Books like these were used in training local organizations, such as the Henrico County Militia of Virginia and the City Troops of Philadelphia. And, of course, there was the "Ancient and Honorable Artillery Company of Boston" that had been organized as early as 1638. Here also flourished "The Train", a rival artillery organization where Henry Knox first learned the use of heavy weapons (Ref 9).

Until the advent of General Steuben's "Blue Book", as it was called by the troops on account of its blue binding, there was no standard, official regulation for the training of the Continental Army. Obviously, the often poorly translated foreign manuals and texts did not make for uniformity in training doctrine. Additionally, every European army possesses a different system of administration and this added to the difficulty in adapting literal translations of their manuals to the American military scene. Von Steuben's strongest point in his work was his adaptation of the Prussian usages to the American character. This quality is reflected throughout his famous manual.

Major General Frederick W. Von Steuben, USA (1730-1794). At Valley Forge, he gave military training and discipline to the citizen-soldiers who achieved the independence of The United States. Author of the first field manual for the United States Army.

*   *   *   *   *

For the first time since Washington had taken command at Cambridge, the American Army was receiving discipline and training at the hands of a professional soldier. Von Steuben's training schedule really constituted the first Infantry School of The United States Army. His insistence upon strict individual and unit discipline and proper and personal leadership of the troops by all the officers was to bring order out of chaos and victory to the American cause. Ensuing operations proved the worth of the old soldier's instruction and his constant emphasis upon the use of the bayonet. Until the appearance of the Baron at Valley Forge, the bayonet had been grossly neglected. The Americans, on the rare occasions when they received issues of beef, used their scarce bayonets as spits for cooking. The following is of interest:

> As a result of von Steuben's drilling, reviews, reports, and inspections, the American Army was, man for man, a match for the best British troops. At Stony Point, an American column stormed the works, with unloaded muskets, and took them at the point of the bayonet. At Guilford Court House, a single regiment of Continentals smashed two enemy regiments, each larger than itself. At Eutaw Springs the Continentals swept the field with the bayonet; and at Yorktown, Alexander Hamilton's column of assault took the enemy redoubt with unloaded muskets and fixed bayonets (Ref 16, p 292).

In the winter after the Battle of Monmouth, General von Steuben in addition to other duties occupied himself and a small staff of young officers with the writing of his famous "Blue Book", or <u>Regulations For The Order and Discipline of the Troops of the United States.</u> This small volume was the first field manual of The United States Army. It was no mere drill manual, although a code of drill regulations formed a part of it. It went much farther; it established a general routine for all military duty, and gave specific instructions for company officers in providing for the general welfare of their commands (Ref 15, p 87).

It contained not only drill and combat doctrine but administrative instructions as well. Basically, it's instructions are as valid today as the day they were put down by the great drillmaster. How the "Blue Book" was written is one of the most interesting sidelights of American military history. According to Colonel Vestal:

> The book was composed in good German by von Steuben; then translated into bad French; then put into good French by Captain Fleury; then translated into poor English by Captain Duponceau; and finally put into good English by Captain Walker. It covered everything necessary in connection with the troops, their weapons, exercises, marches, camps, maneuvers, signal service, inspections, and sick and wounded.

> Von Steuben's Regulations were not in any sense a copy of the Prussian drill regulations. They formed an original book and contained the practical ideas of a man that had met a most difficult problem and had solved it. He established a new arm in the service, the light infantry. The regulations were the crystallization of ideas that he had gained as adjutant general of irregular troops during the Seven Years' War, and his more recent experience with American troops fighting under the special conditions of the terrain in America. Frederick the Great, who carefully studied the American war, introduced light infantry into his own service, from which the idea was adopted by the other European armies. Von Steuben's sanitary regulations are excellent in many respects for use today. Three thousand copies were printed and distributed to the Army. Most of the states reprinted the regulation in 1793 and 1794, in order to carry out the Militia Act of 1792. They were reprinted in 1809 and were used in the War of 1812. Although our drill regulations have been revised many times, the marks of Baron von Steuben are evident on every page, and the spirit remains unchanged (Ref 16, p 290).

Von Steuben laid down specific instructions for officers of all ranks. He established for all time the position of the officer in an army of a democracy. For the first time in the Continental Army, officers were instructed in writing in their duties both in camp and in the field and in winter quarters. The "Blue Book" was a true doctrinal field manual. However, at the same time, it was also an applicatory field manual because it contained specific training information and instruction applicable to men and to units. Von Steuben's "Instructions For The Captain" is a military classic whose validity and usefulness has been proven in every war in which the United States has engaged. To quote von Steuben:

> A Captain cannot be too careful of the company the state has committed to his charge. He must pay the greatest attention to the health of his men, their discipline, arms, accouterments, ammunition, clothes and necessaries. His first object should be to gain the love of his men by treating them with every possible kindness and humanity, inquiring into their complaints, and when well founded, seeing them redressed. He should know every man of his company by name and character. He should often visit those who are sick, speak tenderly to them, see that the public provision, whether medicine or diet, is duly administered, and procure for them besides such comforts and conveniences as are in his power. The attachment that arises from this kind of attention to the sick and wounded is almost inconceivable; it will, moreover, be the means of preserving the lives of many valuable men (Ref 17, App A).

General von Steuben remained in the United States as a citizen after the end of the Revolution. Congress was quick to demonstrate its appreciation for his vital services to the American cause by voting him a life pension of twenty-five hundred dollars a year. The old soldier was also presented with a gold-hilted sword and the several states gave him substantial grants of land. The largest grant of land was located in Oneida County, New York, where the General lived out his days until he died in 1794. In the postwar period, von Steuben remained a close friend of George Washington. Most of his activity centered around the Society of The Cincinnati of which he was a Founder [2].

General von Steuben was one of the first American officers to see the need for systematized military instruction and discipline as essentials to victory in the field. His "Blue Book" synthesized his training, experience and disciplinary code for others. He was one of the first to recognize the requirement of the fledgling republic for a military academy for the formal training of cadets to become officers in the United States Army. The influence of the "drillmaster of Valley Forge" lives on in every field manual published today for the training of the troops of The United States Army. The discipline he brought to the ragged Continentals survives to this day whenever a United States soldier assumes the position of Attention.

---

[2] A patriotic, hereditary membership organization of former Continental officers who like Cincinnatus, the Roman farmer-general, desired to return to peaceful pursuits when victory had been achieved.

At the end of the American Revolution in 1783 the newly independent States through the Continental Congress disbanded the Army and at the same time planned for the defense of the new nation. The military establishment of the United States shrunk to almost nothing with as few as eighty officers and men guarding stores at West Point and at Carlisle, Pennsylvania[3].

Congress on the 2d of June, 1784, resolved:

> That the commanding officer be, and he is hereby directed, to discharge the troops in the service of the United States, except twenty-five privates to guard the stores at Fort Pitt and fifty-five to guard the stores at West Point, and other magazines, with a proportionate number of officers; no officer to remain in service above the rank of captain, and these privates to be retained who were enlisted on the best terms: <u>Provided</u>, that Congress before its recess shall not take other measures respecting the disposition of these troops (Ref 18, pp 68 and 69).

With constant threats of Indian attacks the small regular Army began to develop slowly from a humble beginning. The officer corps was composed primarily of those few veterans who had remained in the service at the close of the Revolution. There was no other source of trained officers until the need caused the establishment of the Military Academy in 1802. Recommended to be established, on a priority basis after the war, by General Washington and General von Steuben and others, the Military Academy was to grow eventually into the first engineering school in the country. Aside from engineering skills, the cadets were taught the elements of war and were fitted to be professional officers in the minute Regular Army of the Republic.

> The initial purpose of the Academy was to train military technicians for all branches of the military service, to encourage the study of military art nationally and thus raise the level of training of the militia, and to encourage the practical study of every science (Ref 19, p 6).

---

[3] At this juncture in our military history it is necessary to point out the inception of the American military policy of dependence upon "volunteer" citizen-soldiers for the defense of the Nation. This concept sprang essentially from the colonists' distrust of large standing armies and the European type civil-military relationship. Hence, the Army was to be small in peacetime. In wartime it was to be augmented by large numbers of "volunteers" and State troops or local militia units.

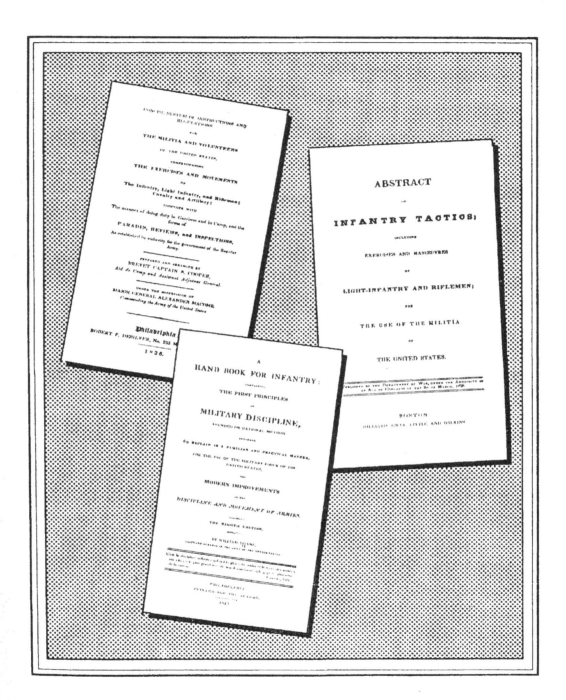

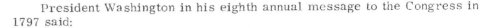

President Washington in his eighth annual message to the Congress in 1797 said:

> The institution of a military academy is also re-
> commended by cogent reasons. However pacific the
> general policy of a nation may be, it ought never to
> be without a stock of military knowledge for emer-
> gencies... (The art of war) demands much previous
> study, and... (knowledge of that art)... in its most
> improved and perfect state is always of great moment
> to the security of a nation... For this purpose an
> academy where a regular course of instruction is
> given is an... expedient which different nations have
> successfully employed (Ref 19, p 5).

The United States Military Academy was founded at West Point, New York, in 1802. It was the flowering of the recommendations made to General Washington by General von Steuben and others at the end of the American Revolution. The training of cadets to become officers in the United States Army was the primary mission of the institution which was to become the repository of military thinking and practice in the United States. It was at West Point where the fledgling military scholars "in time of peace, prepared for war". The early faculty was primarily engineer by pro-fession and mathematics became the solid base of the curriculum.

The introduction of the subject of the United States Military Academy at this juncture is necessary because of the marked influence the institution exerted upon the training and command aspects of the Civil War. After the War of 1812, in which the few graduates served, the Military Academy came under the command of brevet Major Sylvanus Thayer of the Class of 1808 who replaced Captain Alden Partridge, Class of 1806[4]. Superintendent from 1817 to 1833, Thayer broadened the curriculum, adding other subjects in addition to engineering and the mathematical sciences. His influence was so great that he is known as "The Father of the Military Academy". Colonel Thayer is especially significant in relation to the evolution of the US Army field manual in that he was at West Point when many of the future authors were cadets. The scholastic and academic atmosphere engendered at the Academy during Colonel Thayer's tenure was instrumental in developing a small group of graduates who might be termed "military intellectuals". This group was to begin serious professional study of warfare in the United States Army. As faculty members and as authors and commanders and students in the field of warfare they were prime movers in the development of our military doctrinal literature.

First and foremost among the graduated cadets to make his mark in American military science was Dennis Hart Mahan of the Class of 1824. His intellectual attainments placed him at the head of his class and upon

---

[4]See Colonel Lester A. Webb, Captain Alden Partridge and The United States Military Academy, 1806-1833, Northport, Ala.: American Southern, 1965.

CORG-M-244

graduation he was assigned as Assistant Professor of Mathematics and Engineering. After spending a four year tour at the French Military School at Metz, he returned to West Point as Acting Professor and Professor from 1832-1871. The Dictionary of American Biography has this to say about Professor Mahan:

A world-renowned scholar who taught the Science of War to many world-famous graduates (Ref 20, p 210).

But Mahan's influence was to reach far beyond the gray walls of West Point. His writings were to affect the destinies of hundreds of thousands of soldiers who had never seen the Military Academy. Mahan's first effort in the field of American military literature was in the areas of military engineering but his most important work was tactical in scope. Written as texts for the instruction of cadets, Professor Mahan's works such as An Elementary Treatise on an Advanced Guard, Out-post and Detachment Service of Troops and Handling Them in the Presence of an Enemy were invaluable when reprinted by private publishers and made available to the Civil War volunteer officer. Doctrine and practical combat application were to be found in Mahan. These qualities were not often possessed by the available rote-type drill manuals and regulations.

Professor Dennis Hart Mahan (1802-1871). A world renowned scholar who taught the science of war to many famous graduates of the United States Military Academy during the period of 1832-1871. He wrote A Complete Treatise on Field Fortification, 1836; ...Outpost, and Detachment Service of Troops, 1847: Elementary Course of Military Engineering, 1866; Mahan's Permanent Fortifications, 1850, etc.

*   *   *   *   *

Silas Casey of Rhode Island graduated from West Point in the Class of 1826. His early military career was in the Infantry arm and his service included frontier duty, the Florida Indian War, and the Mexican War. Wounded at Chapultepec and brevetted twice for bravery, Casey was noted for his adaptation of the French "Tactics" as translated by William J. Hardee, Class of 1838, for American usage. No intellectual of the school of Thayer and Mahan, Casey was not an author but rather a compiler. However, Casey did contribute to the training literature of the Civil War by adding materials on the corps d'armee to his "Casey's Tactics".

Major General Silas Casey, USA (1807-1882), compiled "Infantry Tactics" which were adopted for use by the US Army in Civil War. Casey's "Tactics" included maneuvers for units of division, corps, and army size.

Silas Casey served in the Civil War as a general officer receiving the rank of brevet Major General of Volunteers. For his Mexican and Civil War services, he received the thanks of the State of Rhode Island. The Dictionary of American Biography credits General Casey's efforts in the drill manual field as follows: Compiled from the French, "Inf Tactics" adopted by the United States in August 1962. His contribution to the training literature of the Civil War was considerable. The "Tactics" which he compiled after Hardee were highly essential manuals for the Infantry of the Union Army. His addition of the part pertaining to the division and the corps d'armee were of vital importance to the officers in command of major units in the field. The Army Corps, consisting of two or more divisions, was not American in concept. It had been adopted from the French who, in turn, received it as a military legacy from Napoleon Bonaparte (Ref 6, pp 41-43).

* * * * *

* * * * *

William J. Hardee entered the Dragoons (US Mounted Rifles) after graduation from West Point in 1838. After serving for two years in the Florida Indian War, he was sent abroad to attend the French Cavalry School at Saumur, France. His subsequent career in the Mexican War was distinguished by the receipt of two brevets for bravery in the field. In 1855, he translated the French "Tactics" for American use. His translation carried out the French manual to include the school of the battalion. As noted, Silas Casey revised Hardee at the beginning of the Civil War, Colonel Hardee, former Commandant of Cadets at West Point, having "gone South" to become a Lieutenant General in the Confederate Army. Hardee's "Tactics" as revised by Casey were not only the

Lieutenant General William J. Hardee, CSA, (1815-1873). While a Lieutenant Colonel was author of Hardee's Tactics before the Civil War. The Tactics were used extensively by both the North and the South during the Civil War.

principal infantry field manual of the Union infantry, it was also reprinted from the 1855 edition for the use of the Confederate troops in the South.

Next to Professor Dennis Hart Mahan, Henry Wager Halleck was perhaps the most distinguished American in the field of military studies prior to the Civil War. Halleck graduated in the Class of 1839, served with distinction in the Mexican War, and resigned as a Captain in 1854. Entering the legal profession in California he developed a highly successful law practice while maintaining his interest in the military profession in the California militia. His writings, which he continued in civil life, were noted for translations of Jomini's Theory of War and The Life of Napoleon. He also produced works on International Law and the Law of War which are standard authorities today.

Major General Henry W. Halleck (1815-1872). Author of military textbooks on war. Chief of Staff, USA, 1864-65. General-in-Chief, USA, 1862-1864.

*　　*　　*　　*　　*

Halleck's Elements of Military Art and Science was published privately, first in 1846, while the author-translator was in active service. Based largely upon his thorough knowledge of Jominian tactics, Halleck produced a work that was to influence American tactical doctrine until after the Civil War. Reissued by a civilian firm in 1861, when the Volunteer officers were literally crying for training and doctrinal literature, the reprint did not allow for the twenty-year gap in infantry weapons development. The improved lethality of the .58 caliber percussion cap rifled musket, firing the Minie bullet, over the .69 caliber flintlock smoothbore musket was not noted in the new edition. As a consequence, Civil War tactical doctrine generally followed the mass principle advocated by Napoleon and transmitted to the Americans by well-known translations of Jomini (Ref 7, pp 64 and 65).

The absence of any other authoritative treatise on tactical doctrine gave the product of "Old Brains" Halleck, as he was familiarly known, a secure place in the saddlebags of the new colonels and generals. The President of the United States, Abraham Lincoln, brought the resigned 1854 Regular Army captain to Washington and appointed him General-in-Chief of the US Armies. In 1864, he was made Chief of Staff under General U.S. Grant. The Dictionary of American Biography states "He greatly improved discipline throughout Federal Armies" (Ref 20, p 225).

Thus it will be seen that the Military Academy performed an essential service for the new nation in becoming from the very beginning the fountain-head of the military profession in the United States. With the mission of training young men to become officers the Academy must, of necessity, possess the resources and means to impart such education and training. In the course of establishing its curriculum, West Point, through its leaders, visited and inspected the finest military educational institutions of Europe.

It was a natural consequence that the materials collected abroad, or written for the instruction at West Point, would have a salient effect upon the American military profession and its training literature. Lectures and exercises delivered at the Academy became the military doctrine for the evolving Regular Army and its units in the field. The instructors and professors at the Military Academy were among the first Americans to become proficient in translation of the military art of the world into American usage.

> Our national Military Academy, founded at the instance
> of the great men of the Revolutionary era, has grown with
> our growth, has kept up in our midst a thorough knowledge
> of the military profession, and has given us competent
> commanders for any force we have found it necessary to
> use, from the small detachment sent in pursuit of the
> hostile Indian, to the vast hosts marshalled under a single
> banner during our greatest war (The Civil War) (Ref 18,
> p 90, parentheses added).

From 1802 to 1846, the beginning of the Mexican War, the Military Academy had graduated 1,330 cadets [5]. Their influence upon the military art in America was to be considerable and their effect upon civil life and civil engineering was to be marked. An effort at standardization of the American military profession was attempted at West Point and its effect carried into the military service by the graduates. The effect of West Point upon the field of military literature was noted early. This was especially true in the area of translation of the French manuals by officers who had studied French at the Academy. Those young officers of the highest accomplishment were often ordered abroad as observers and as students at foreign military schools. Their perception of what was valuable was often adapted to American military usage and became a vital part of our written training materials and military literature.

> To the casual student it might seem that until about
> 1860 West Point was filling the almost dual roles of
> national military academy and of national school of civil
> engineering. But despite the curricular emphasis on
> civil engineering and the renown of her graduates in that
> field, the Academy never forgot her deepest and most

---

[5] Register of Graduates and Former Cadets of the United States Military Academy, West Point Alumni Foundation, Inc., 1963.

abiding obligation to the Nation: to send forth graduates trained in the art and science of war. That the obligation was fulfilled is attested for these early years by the records of the Mexican and Civil Wars. The record of the Mexican War is told best in the words of General Winfield Scott: "I give it as my fixed opinion, that but for our graduated cadets, the war between the United States and Mexico might, and probably would, have lasted some four or five years, with, in its first half, more defeats than victories falling to our share; whereas, in less than two campaigns, we conquered a great country and a peace, without the loss of a single battle or skirmish" (Ref 19, p 9).

Thus, it will be seen that, from the very beginning of the Republic, American military training doctrine as exemplified in the published manuals was influenced heavily by what Europe afforded. When the small Regular Army was attempting to create an American military profession the faculty at West Point was instrumental in converting European military training doctrine to American use. As educated gentlemen, at a time when education was rare, the graduates exemplified advance literacy and scholarship. This excellence was found not only in the military and engineering professions but in the areas of teaching and text book writing. The translation of foreign military manuals and the attempted writing of original ones was a concomittant product of the pedagogical talent developed at West Point from 1802 until the beginning of the Civil War in 1861. Other than those manuals produced by the Scott Board, the rest, with few exceptions, were the products of the efforts of Academy graduates.

This period, while marked by considerable intellectual activity on the parts of the graduates both out in the service and at the Academy, produced little original military tactical thought. Other than those tactics which had been "borrowed" from the French, there was nothing new tactically in the American military profession. The influence of Napoleon and his interpreter, General Antoine Henri Jomini, was too profound to be modified. It was not until after the end of the Civil War that an American, Emory Upton, Class of 1861, dared break away from the Napoleonic tradition of mass infantry attacks and create a new dimension in tactical patterns -- the infantry rifle squad[6].

THE AMERICAN CIVIL WAR (1861-1865)

In 1860 the small regular army was scattered over the states and territories. Usually it was engaged in Indian campaigns or performing

---

[6]Brevet Major General Emory Upton, A New System of Infantry Tactics Double and Single Rank Adapted to American Topography and Improved Firearms, New York: D. Appleton & Company, 1867.

garrison duties along the Eastern and Western seacoasts. Generally, such activity did not bring forth noteworthy intellectual achievements in military theory or practice. Yet, the period between the war with Mexico (1846-1848) and the Civil War did produce several influential American professional military writers. Several of these soldier-authors and compilers or translators, were to exert considerable influence upon the development and conduct of training and battle tactics in both the Union and Confederate Armies. Drill Regulations prior to 1861 were those promulgated by successive Boards of Officers such as the one as early as 1826 headed by General Winfield Scott.

A board of officers consisting of Generals Scott and Swift and Colonels Fenwick, Cumming, and Drayton, who had been ordered "conformable to the House of Representatives" to prepare a set of Infantry Drill Regulations "after the pattern of the Rules and Regulations for the Field Service and Maneuvers of the French Infantry," now submitted the results of their labor. This was the first work of its kind actually prepared by a regularly constituted board of American officers (Ref 13, p 143).

In 1834, General Scott adapted the Prussian tactical system to the United States Army. Henceforth, the Manual was familiarly known as "Scott's Tactics." This system of drill and tactical exercises obtained within the United States Army until the advent of new infantry weapons. The improvement of firearms, the change of the ignition system from flintlock to the weatherproof percussion lock and the invention of the highly accurate base-expanding bullet by Captain Minie of the French Army demanded a new and improved infantry drill and tactical manual. There was none forthcoming until after the war.

*   *   *   *   *

Brevet Lieutenant General Winfield Scott, USA, (1786-1866). Distinguished general officer and author of manuals on tactics for Infantry and Artillery. He was one of the first to see the need for professional training literature in the US Army.

At the beginning of the American Civil War the greatest need was training doctrine covering organization and employment of small and large bodies of troops; that is, as small as a company and as large as a division, an army corps, or a field army. As noted, there was little or no such material available except the privately or commercially published works of a very small group of professional officers or former officers of the United States Army. The Drill Regulations were adequate for teaching the school of the soldier, dismounted,

24

with and without arms. The drill evolutions of the company and battalion were included in the translated French drill regulations to be found in "Hardee's Tactics" and "Casey's Tactics". At this point, it must be emphasized that during this period the drill manual of the parade ground was the drill manual of the battle field. There had been little or no attempt to create a separate and distinct combat drill for use in the field. The Zouave drill, taken from the tactics noted by American observers in the French Colonial troops in Algiers and elsewhere in Africa, did feature extended order and skirmish drills. This was a realistic approach to combat but all United States troops were not trained as Zouaves - only a limited number of state and privately sponsored units followed the system (Ref 21, pp 39 and 40).

General Winfield Scott traveled extensively in Europe and his tactical works were translations from and adaptations of the French system of training and combat operations. As one of the senior, and eventually the senior, general officer of the United States Army, General Scott's appreciation and approbation of French military institutions contributed to their popularity in this country.

With the influx of hundreds of thousands of Volunteers, the Government Printing Office in Washington could not hope to supply the demand for training literature, that is, drill regulations and manuals. Private publishers, such as Lippincott of Philadelphia, Harpers, and Van Nostrand of New York were the more prominent ones and they poured forth for the commercial market a flood of manuals on every conceivable military subject. Old manuals were resurrected and brought forth for the eager Volunteer, both officer and man, who had to learn a new profession in which he would be an amateur until he had gained professional experience. Often carrying the line "By Authority", these volumes were accepted by the average officer and soldier as "official doctrine" which they were often not! Casey's "Tactics", privately printed by Van Nostrand, was officially adopted in 1862 as the regulation drill manual and guide for infantry training of the wartime United States Army (Ref 21, p 40).

The dearth of training manuals at the beginning of the Civil War was remedied somewhat by the reprinting of the works of Hardee, Casey, Mahan, and Halleck. Printed commercially, these manuals were the "bibles" of the Volunteer officer and soldier. In format these books were generally of a size to fit the soldier's pocket and pack or the field officer's saddlebag. Many were profusely illustrated in order to communicate the ideas to an often not too literate reader audience. Diagrams and plates showing the various movements and positions in the manual of arms and company movements were always included. Details of precision were worked out for parades and inspection formations. Other than Army Regulations which contained little tactical doctrine, few of the publications emanated from the Government Printing Office in Washington.

The French influence which had permeated American tactical doctrine since the days of The Scott Board in 1826 and continued by Halleck, McClellan, Hardee, and Casey, persisted in the outpourings of the manual

EXTRACT FROM AN ACT PROVIDING FOR THE PRINTING AND BINDING SIXTY THOUSAND COPIES OF THE ABSTRACT OF INFANTRY TACTICS, INCLUDING MANŒUVRES OF LIGHT-INFANTRY AND RIFLEMEN, AND FOR OTHER PURPOSES.

Be it enacted by the Senate and House of Representatives of the United States of America in Congress assembled, That the Secretary of War be, and he is hereby, authorized and directed, to contract with HILLIARD, GRAY AND CO. of Boston, or some other person or persons, for printing, binding and delivering, sixty thousand copies of the Abstract of Infantry Tactics, including Exercises and Manœuvres of Light-Infantry and Riflemen, for the Use of the Militia of the United States; also, five thousand copies of a System of Exercise and Instruction of Field-Artillery, including Manœuvres for Light or Horse-Artillery; as reported by the Secretary of War, on the eighth of January, eighteen hundred and twenty-seven; agreeably to the proposals of said HILLIARD, GRAY AND CO., made to the Secretary of War, dated on the twenty-seventh of October, eighteen hundred and twenty-seven, in their specimen marked B: and when so printed, bound and delivered, the Secretary of War is hereby directed to apportion the same among the several States and Territories, and in the District of Columbia, for the use of the Militia thereof, according to the number of the Militia in each State and Territory and the District of Columbia; and to forward to the Chief Magistrate of each State and Territory the number allowed to such State and Territory as aforesaid, to be by said Chief Magistrate distributed among the officers of the Militia of such State or Territory, for their use, and the use of their successors in office, under such rules and regulations as they may direct. And the Secretary of War will cause the number of copies apportioned to the District of Columbia to be distributed among the officers of the Militia in the District, under such rules and regulations as may be prescribed by the President of the United States.

Approved 2d of March, 1829.

NOTICE.

HILLIARD, GRAY AND CO., BOSTON, will supply States, Booksellers, and others, with this Work, and also the System of Artillery Exercise, in any quantity, on the most liberal terms.

WASHINGTON, Dec. 5, 1826.

SIR,

THE Board of Officers assembled at this place, under your orders of October 5, 1826, for, among other purposes, reporting "*A System of Instruction for the Militia Infantry,*" have now the honor to submit, through its Recorder, (Lieutenant Eakin,) the annexed sheets.

We have the honor to be,

Sir,

With high respect,

Your most ob't servants,

WINFIELD SCOTT,
Maj. Gen. and President of the Board.

T. CADWALADER,
Maj. Gen. Penn. Militia.

WM. H. SUMNER,
Adj. Gen. of Massachusetts.

B. DANIEL,
Adj. Gen. Militia, North Carolina.

ABRM. EUSTIS,
Lieut. Col. 4th Artillery.

Z. TAYLOR,
Lieut. Col. 1st Regt. U. S. Infantry.

G. CUTLER,
Lieut. Col. 2d Infantry.

CHARLES J. NOURSE,
U. S. A.

To the
HON. JAMES BARBOUR,

Secretary of War.

translators and writers. The French Zouave system of light infantry skirmish drill was especially liked by the Volunteer officer who needed a new departure to and short cut for training his unit. The militia, or State troops, were especially attracted to the Zouave system and there were Zouave units without limit. One of the most famous of the Zouave organizations was the precision drill unit organized before the Civil War by Colonel Elmer E. Ellsworth as the United States Zouave Cadets. Winning first prizes in many of the State militia drill competitions, the Zouave Cadets publicized the Zouave system. With the Civil War, Ellsworth and his Zouaves were mobilized and the young commander's drill manual became popular in the training of the other Zouave organizations. Colonel Ellsworth was killed at Alexandria, Virginia, early in the war when he tried to prevent a Rebel sympathizer from hauling down the United States flag. His system of precision drill was adopted by innumerable state and militia units coming into the service. If Ellsworth had lived, the Zouave system would have been used more generally throughout the United States Army.

The Napoleonic concept of war dominated the military literature of the American Civil War on both sides. This was due partially to the perpetuation of the Napoleonic tactics through the translations made of the various French military works. The most basic reason for the concept's survival was in the fact that Napoleon had commanded large masses of troops and the Civil War became a struggle almost immediately involving armies of a size never before witnessed in the United States. The study of the campaigns of Napoleon at the Military Academy and elsewhere in the service had created a professional military approach based upon an assumption that successful battles of the historic past could be recreated on similar terrain with total disregard of weapon advancement at a later date. Commanders were wont to ask themselves, "What did Napoleon do in a similar situation at Borodino, Wagram, or Ratisbon?" The following comment by Brigadier General Thomas Jordan, C.S.A.[7] illustrates how worship of the tactics of the "Little Corporal" influenced the Battle of Shiloh in April 1862.

> As I framed this order, I had before me Napoleon's order for the battle of Waterloo, and, in attention to ante-battle details, took those of such soldiers as Napoleon and (Marshal) Soult for model - a fact which I have mentioned because the ante-Shiloh has been hypercriticised" (Ref 22, pp 594-603).

Such slavish addiction to the Napoleonic tactical concept did not permit much innovation. But above and beyond this serious fault the fact that weaponry had been improved and made more accurate and deadly was overlooked to the point where the tactics were at least half a century behind the progress in infantry and artillery armament.

---

[7] Class of 1840, West Point

The old manuals of pre-Civil War days by Hardee, Cooper, Scott and others were brought out and republished commercially. Many of these were valuable for foot drill but were not brought up-to-date with the weaponry of the times. Halleck's works on military science written in the 1840's were reprinted without regard to the fact that infantry weaponry had become more accurate and so more lethal. The mass infantry attack theories of Napoleon, as expounded by Jomini and translated by Halleck, were thus presented as tactical doctrine when, in fact, they were at least twenty-five years out of date. The largest mobilization faced by the nation up to that time, the Civil War required tactical combat doctrine that called for the maneuver of divisions, army corps, and armies. There was little of large unit tactics in the manuals available to the United States Army.

Casey's "Tactics" was unique in that it did contain translation of the French doctrine for the maneuver of the division and the army corps. There was little available anywhere on the techniques of commanding an army in the field. The following comment of General Irwin McDowell, the Union commander at the Battle of Bull Run, is highly significant of the situation facing the commanders of the hurriedly mobilized divisions and corps:

> There was not a man there who had ever maneu-
> vered troops in large bodies. There was not one in
> the Army. I did not believe there was one in the whole
> country. At least, I knew there was no one there who
> had ever handled 30,000 troops. I had seen them
> handled abroad in reviews and marches, but I had
> never handled that number, and no one here had (Ref
> 13, pp 256 and 257).

The manuals were generally French in origin as far as tactics and drill were concerned. How faithfully the Union Army had copied the French Army system is shown in the comments of General F. V. A. de Chanal, a French Army observer with the Federal forces during the Civil War. General de Chanal noted:

> Our methods have been copied very exactly. It
> will be readily seen that the American troops having
> been continually in a state of war, can not in matters
> of drill be compared to European troops. Those
> organizations, however, which were drilled in the
> various forts and depots before joining the army, are
> well enough instructed (Ref 23, p 26).

It should be noted at this point that the remarks of General de Chanal reflect the training situation he observed within the Federal Army. The Zouave system was, in effect, the precise close-order and extended skirmish drill used by certain French corps of light troops in the campaigns in Algiers. It was in great contrast to the regular infantry drill, which was simple close-order drill, which had to suffice for both the parade ground and the battlefield. Infantry close-order drill, as described in the manuals mentioned previously, became the basic training vehicle for combat in the field. The old manuals and the mass combat tactics of Napoleon were about the only sources of military training available to the hastily organized troops.

Major General George B. McClellan, USA, (1826-1885). Author of Manual of Bayonet Exercise, Regulations and Instructions for the Field Service of the United States Cavalry in Time of War. General-in-Chief of Armies of the United States, 1861-1862.

General George B. McClellan of the Class of 1846 was considered one of the most promising young officers of the pre-Civil War regular army. His experience in Europe and the Crimea had been reflected in his report to the War Department. Later, in 1851, he translated a Manual of the Bayonet Exercise by M. Comard, an eminent French teacher of the art of fencing. Printed "by order of the War Department" and sold privately, the Manual of the Bayonet Exercise was reprinted during the Civil War as a popular manual.

The Government Printing Office was neither equipped nor manned to handle the tremendous volume of printed manuals required for the Army and Navy. The effect of the war upon the public printer may be noted in the following extract:

*   *   *   *   *

Government printing orders mushroomed. Presses jammed every corner. Machines in private shops were rented. Paper doubled, trebled in cost, and became almost unobtainable, and in 1864 sold for $560 a ton. Printers demanded $24 a week. A private firm lent payroll money to the GPO.

... The war years created a scarcity of paper and printing ink in both North and South. The South particularly felt the pinch, because paper, ink, and type had to come from the North. In the South, newspapers were reduced in size, headlines were omitted, and frantic appeals were made for rags and materials for making paper. In some cases, wrapping paper and the

blank side of wall paper were used, with shoe blacking
serving as improvised ink. In the Confederate States,
many printers were exempted from military services
(Ref 24, p 36).

It was into this printing vacuum that the commercial printers and
publishers threw their resources. The demand for military texts and
manuals was so great that many of the old-line publishers added a
"military" line in their production and sales plans. Among these well-
known publishing houses were Harpers, Lippincott, and Van Nostrand.
In addition, there were other small publishers and printers who contributed to the outpouring of military literature. From the amount produced
it appears that the private printers were in much better position with
reference to paper and ink than the Government Printing Office. It should
be noted that as the Government Printing Office opened on March 4, 1861,
the same day Abraham Lincoln was inaugurated, it had no time to create
a stockpile of printing supplies and materials.

Among those publishing firms mentioned, the house of Van Nostrand
appears to have been preferred, as Van Nostrand was designated as the
"official publisher for the United States Army and Navy". According to
Lord in his book, They Fought For the Union, David Van Nostrand even
before 1861

> ...had gone into the publishing of military
> and naval books in earnest. When the war broke out,
> his friendship with such men as Brigadier General
> J. G. Barnard [8] and others was continued and these
> men prepared some excellent professional monographs
> and books which were published by Van Nostrand who
> became the "official publisher for the United States
> Army and Navy. His business cards, preserved in
> the publishing company's archives carry that phrase
> ...At the outbreak of the war, the US Army was
> lacking a satisfactory system of infantry drill; this
> need was supplied by Brigadier General Silas Casey,
> whose system of "tactics", published in 1862 by Van
> Nostrand, was adopted as the standard guide for train-
> ing the United States Army. It was also reproduced
> in Richmond and used by the C.S. Army (Ref 21, p 40).

J. B. Lippincott and Company of Philadelphia also printed a large
number of manuals for the Armed forces during the Civil War. While
Lippincott is noted as having concentrated in the field of military surgical
manuals and texts, the firm did publish in 1862 a comprehensive list of
military manuals (see App B).

---

[8]Class of 1833, West Point, Superintendent, USMA, 1855-1866.

Harper and Brothers of New York shared a goodly portion of the manual publishing business beginning with General Winfield Scott's Infantry Tactics, in three volumes, which was released in 1861 at the start of the Federal mobilization. This manual was a popular one with the Volunteer officers and men. Winfield Scott was highly regarded by the general public and his name on the title page of a manual meant authenticity. Among well-known competitors in the military manual publishing field were D. Appleton, Putnam and Sons, and John Wiley of New York City who brought out reprints of Mahan's basic works. In the South, editions of Hardee were published at Richmond. Another edition was published in Mobile, Alabama, by S. H. Goetzel in 1863. The Trooper's Manual by Colonel J. Lucius Davis, C.S.A., of the Class of 1833, West Point, was published by A. Morris in Richmond in 1862. Appleton's major publishing effort was in the bringing forth of a new, but not revised, edition of Henry Wager Halleck's Elements of Military Science, first published in 1846. As noted previously, this book probably influenced the tactical and strategical operations of the Federal Armies as much or more than any other contemporary military treatise.

Ganoe makes the following observation on the training provided by the infantry manuals of the Civil War period:

> Although the Federal militia had in many cases its own state drill, Scott's drill regulations were reprinted in three parts for immediate use. Apparently there were no changes over the regulations issued in 1835. The company drilled in two ranks and loaded "in twelve times". With the comparatively few weapons having percussion caps and with the breechloaders, the motions for loading were reduced to nine and less. After the recruit had passed through the "school of the soldier" he was required to be instructed in "target firing". The records of the corporals and privates, who fired from 3 to 5 rounds per day, were kept for the purpose of dividing the soldiers into three classes; "The most excellent marksmen, the next in accuracy, the most indifferent". The largest part of the ammunition was required to be expended on the last class (Ref 13, p 266).

With reference to the heavy artillery arm of the Civil War Federal forces, the following extract from Ganoe indicates the state of the art at that time. What is noted about the Union Army may be applied with equal validity to the Confederate artillery.

> A manual on "Heavy Artillery", as intricate as it was elaborate, showed the juvenile state of our readiness. Guns of every type, irrespective of their peculiarities, were treated of because they had to be used. There were 8-inch howitzers on 24-pounder siege carriages; 10-inch siege mortars, coehorn mortars, 10-inch seacoast mortars, 13-inch seacoast mortars,

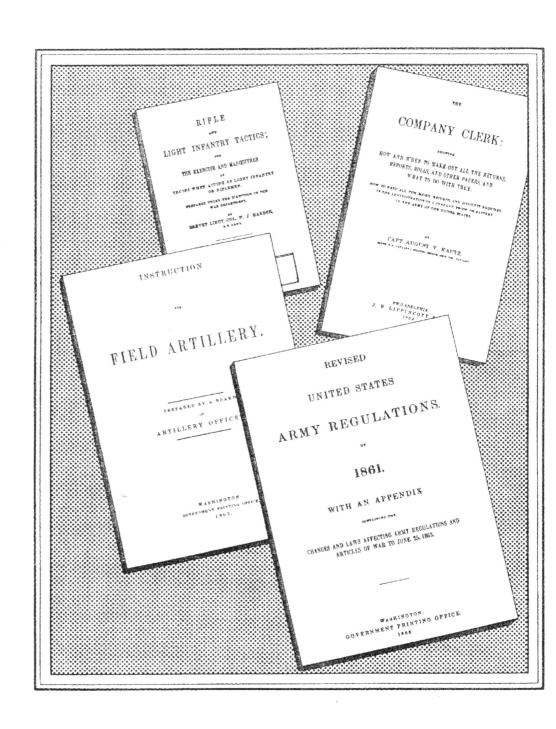

stone mortars, 8-inch seacoast howitzers on barbette carriages; 10-inch seacoast howitzers on barbette carriages; 8-inch columbiads on casemate carriages; 24-pounder howitzers on flank casemate carriages; 8-inch columbiads on columbiad carriages; and 10-inch columbiads on columbiad carriages. Nor were these all the types that were brought into play. All heavy weapons that could be scraped together had to be called into service whether or not they were appropriate. No wonder the cannoneer was required to understand the service of the piece in field artillery before taking up the heavy (Ref 13, p 266).

As early as 1836, Wiley and Long had published Dennis Hart Mahan's A Complete Treatise On Field Fortification and, in 1847, Wiley distributed Mahan's famous Out-Post and Detachment Service of Troops and Handling Them in the Presence of an Enemy manual. The Field Fortification treatise was revised and reissued in 1863 [9]. Next to those of Halleck and Casey, the writings of Mahan exerted the most influence upon tactics and strategy. His effect upon the leadership of both sides especially was significant because of his long service as a professor at the Military Academy. During this period many of the higher-ranking general officers of both Armies had been taught as cadets by Mahan and they were familiar with his theories of warfare (Ref 7, pp 65 and 66).

There was yet another badly neglected field of military instruction which was to exert a considerable effect upon the well-being and care of the individual soldier. This was unit administration, that is, military bookkeeping, the maintaining of the unit records and returns in an efficient and soldierly manner. This skill the Volunteers did not possess initially. At the beginning of the war there were not enough forms printed by the Government Printing Office for issue to the newly forming units [10]. The old Regular Army officers and men were well acquainted with the mysteries of the Morning Report, the Sick Book, the Ration Return, and the Requisition but the new officers and noncommissioned officers soon were entwined by the hopeless tangle of military "red tape" as it was termed from the red cloth binder used to tie and wrap the completed forms.

One of the interesting aspects of command during the Civil War was the method used by commanders to urge their subordinates to buy and to read the manuals published and sold commercially. In the absence of official doctrine these texts served as basic instruction in the art of war.

----

[9] In 1861, Mahan's "Outpost" was published in New Orleans by Bloomfield & Steel. In 1862, the Richmond publishing house of West & Johnson printed an edition of "Field Fortification" for the Confederate Army.

[10] U.S. Grant, as an ex-Captain of the Regular Army, West Point Class of 1843, was engaged in ruling blank forms and acting as drillmaster for the Volunteer troops at the State Capitol in Springfield, Illinois, in 1861.

Time was pressing and the hastily assembled Volunteers, officers and men, often had no combat training other than that gained in bivouac while marching to the troop concentration area.

In 1863, Lippincott of Philadelphia published The Company Clerk by Colonel and Brevet Major General August V. Kautz, Class of 1852, West Point. This little volume showed the amateur soldier clerk and commander how to satisfy the precise and exacting demands of Army paperwork. The title page carried the happy answer to the harrassed company clerk's prayer: "How and When To Make Out all the Returns, Reports, Rolls, and Other Papers, and What to Do With Them". With the added burden of facing the mounting flood of reports, records, and other administrative papers, as well as facing the enemy, this volume received whole-hearted endorsement by all. In fact, some commanders gave the manual their official blessing and urged their officers to purchase it. The following extract Circular tells the story:

CIRCULAR

HEAD-QUARTERS DISTRICT OF COLUMBUS

6th DIVISION, 16th ARMY CORPS

Columbus, Ky., June 28, 1863

The attention of Company Officers is called to a lately published work, by J. B. Lippincott & Co., of Philadelphia, entitled:

"THE COMPANY CLERK: showing how and when to make out all the Returns, Reports, Rolls, and other Papers, and what to do with them. How to keep all the Books, Records, and Accounts required in the Administration of a Company, Troop, or Battery in the Army of the United States. By Captain August V. Kautz, 6th U.S. Cavalry; Colonel 2d Ohio Vol. Cavalry."

This work can be purchased at the bookstores in Columbus and Cairo, at St. Louis, &c.: and all officers in the volunteer service are recommended to acquaint themselves with its very valuable and necessary information.

By order of Brigadier-General Asboth

T. H. Harris,
Assistant Adjutant-General
(Ref 25).

The Revised U.S. Army Regulations 1863 were published in spite of the cited shortage of paper by the Government Printing Office as one of the major wartime printing projects. This heavy volume of 594 pages contained nearly complete information with which to command a military organization. But, as always, the "Regulations" did not cover in detail the finer points of leadership, command, and administration. Often they were vague and mysterious in their meaning to the raw Volunteer officer and noncommissioned officer. Hence, there arose a need for their interpretation by "experts" who had lived with them for years in the time of peace. Such an example of this interpretation has been cited as The Company Clerk written by Colonel Kautz. While the Regulations indicated the duties of the company clerk they did NOT show him how to perform them. This, Colonel Kautz's book endeavored to accomplish in the interest of better and more efficient company, troop, and battery administration. Although the "Regulations" did not cover tactical operations in detail, they did establish general doctrine and vague principles for the conduct of a battle. The following paragraph is an example:

> 728. In battles and military operations it is better to assume the offensive, and put the enemy on the defensive; but to be safe in doing so requires a larger force than the enemy, or better troops, and favorable ground. When obliged to act on the defensive, the advantage of position and of making the attack may sometimes be secured by forming in rear of the ground on which we are to fight, and advancing at the moment of action. In mountain warfare, the assailant has always the disadvantage; and even in offensive warfare in the open field, it may frequently be very important, when the artillery is well posted, and any advantage of the ground may be secured, to await the enemy and compel him to attack (Ref 26, p 105).

Major General George B. McClellan, translator from the French of the Bayonet Exercise For the Army, brought forth a manual for the mounted service entitled Regulations and Instructions For The Field Service of The United States Cavalry in Time of War, 1861. Published by Lippincott of Philadelphia it

> ...dealt with the conduct of marches and the duties of commanders of "the advanced guard, rear guard, flank guard and rear detachments". It treated at great length the subjects of outposts, patrols, videttes, pickets and main guards. Columns and wheelings of two and fours in open order came into being with this work and added to the facility of movement of cavalry. The terms dragoon and mounted rifles now disappeared. All mounted troops were called cavalry (Ref 13, p 267).

This work was significant in that it amplified Mahan's "Outpost" treatise and applied many of his principles to the mounted service. However, Mahan's was still a basic text in the area of field service and it remained so for the duration of the Civil War. As McClellan had been a pupil of Mahan while at West Point, there is every reason to believe that the great teacher of the tactics of war influenced General McClellan's thinking in this area of the military profession. McClellan was in reality an engineer and had served as an engineer officer in the Mexican War. His experience with the mounted arm dated from his assignment to the 1st Cavalry Regiment and his membership on the Board of United States Officers which visited the Crimean War front and Europe 1855-1856. Returning to the United States in April 1856, the Board made an extended and most complete printed report. The military information contained therein was to exert a profound influence upon the United States Army. As an example of this influence the McClellan saddle, designed by Captain McClellan from those he observed in the Crimea and Europe, has survived to the present time (Ref 15, p 235).

In the pre-Civil War United States mounted service, the general drill and tactics were British in origin. Contrasted to the Infantry, the Cavalry owed its operational patterns to the British and not to the French. The post-Revolutionary War United States Army did adopt a mounted service during the War of 1812 in which hurriedly raised mounted units had served and then disbanded. In 1833, The First Regiment of Mounted Rifles was formed and the Second Regiment's organization followed in 1836. Primarily established to counter the high mobility of the pony-mounted Indian of the Great Plains, the Dragoon, as he was called, was in reality a mounted infantryman. The following comment by A. S. K. Brown in the introduction to Nesmith's Soldier's Manual is significant:

> Unlike those for infantry, the cavalry manuals generally derived from British sources. The "six cuts" of the sword exercise first appeared, complete with engraved diagram superimposed on a human face, in the Rules and Regulations for the Sword Exercise of the Cavalry published for the War Office by T. Egerton in 1796. The first American edition of this work edited by Robert Hewes, was published in Boston in 1802, and was subsequently revised and republished by Craig in Baltimore in 1812 (Ref 12, p iv).

In 1799 at Abraham Lodge, Halifax, William Richardson Davis, Esquire, published Instructions to be Observed for the Formations and Movements of the Cavalry. In 1822, Pierce Darrow wrote Cavalry Tactics which was published by Oliver D. Cooke, in Hartford, Connecticut. Earlier in 1801 E. A. Jenks published in Portland, Maine, Cavalry Exercise Containing Instruction for the American Cavalry. By 1834, Cavalry, Light Infantry and Rifle Tactics was published by authority of The War Department. In 1826, General Winfield Scott headed a board of officers, consisting of himself as president and with several militia generals as members, which produced Cavalry Tactics. This work was especially detailed and covered the essentials of cavalry drill and tactical maneuvers. As there were no cavalry units in the regular army at this time, this book was written especially for the mounted units of the various state militia organizations.

> There now being no cavalry in the service, it's maneuvers had to be kept alive solely by regulations

for the volunteers. Lieutenant Colonel Pierce Darrow accordingly adapted such a work to Scott's regulations, calling it Cavalry Tactics. He confessed at the beginning that the organization of a cavalry regiment was so radically different in most of the states that it was quite impossible to give a standard type. He compromised, however, by laying down "the order of formation" for two regiments of different size. He conformed to the law of 1820 in prescribing that regiments should be called battalions, and that the companies should be posted in line according to the dates of the captains' commissions (Ref 13, p 161).

Most of the artillery manuals of the Civil War were, like those of the infantry, based upon the French system. From the earliest days of the Continental Army's General Henry Knox and his artillery, instruction and training in the horse artillery, or mobile field artillery, rested upon either British or French sources. During the War of 1812 period, the artillery tactics of the Army were based upon the works of General Thaddeus Kosciusko, the highly skilled engineer and brilliant Polish soldier who came to help the struggling colonists. His "Exercises for cannon and field ordnance" and "Maneuvers for horse artillery" were the property of the West Point Philosophical Society of the Military Academy. The United States purchased the copy from the Philosophical Society for the sum of $200 and ordered the contents printed as the governing regulations for the artillery of the United States Army. Birkhimer in his definitive work, Historical Sketch of The Artillery, United States Army quotes the official letter of the War Department:

War Department, August 1st, 1812

The exercises for cannon and field ordnance and manoeuvres for horse artillery, as altered from the manual of General Kosciusko and adapted to the service of the United States, are hereby ordered for the government of the several corps of artillery in the said service. Such alterations and improvements as experience may suggest will be reported to the several commanding officers of regiments, and by them to the Department of War.

The Government gave the West Point Philosophical Society $200 for the copyright of Kosciusko's manoeuvres thus appropriated (Ref 10, p 301).

Hence, it is noted that there was no distinct American artillery doctrine, as such, until the Civil War where it was developed in the field by skilled gunners of the type of Brevet Brigadier General Henry Hunt, Chief of Artillery of the Army of The Potomac. Various translations of the French artillery tactics continued to appear as late as 1826 when Lieutenant Daniel Tyler's translation of the French manual was approved by the war department and published to the service in 1829 as A System of Exercise and Instruction of Field Artillery. Captain Robert Anderson, of later Fort Sumter fame, translated from the French, Instruction For Field Artillery, Horse and Foot and adapted it in 1845 to the United States Army artillery. By 1858, a board of professional artillerists of the United States Army convened to devise doctrine and technique for field artillery[11]. After meeting for two years the board submitted its recommendations which were approved and incorporated in a new manual, Instruction for Field Artillery, which was adopted as regulation by the War Department in 1860. It was published by Lippincott of Philadelphia in 1861. Lord in his work, They Fought For The Union, commented upon this manual and its time-liness:

> The appearance of this manual, only before the outbreak of war was extremely fortunate for the Union cause. As is well known, the excellent regular and volunteer batteries of the Federal army made the difference in several critical battles of the war. Certainly some of the credit for their brilliant combat record must go to the excellent training they received, a training based on the 1860 manual (Ref 21, p 67).

Another professional artillerist who contributed to the development of tactics for that arm was Brigadier General (later Brevet Major General) John Gibbon of the Class of 1847, West Point. Both Gibbon and Hunt departed from the stereotype of French Army artillery systems and contributed methods which were essentially new and advanced in tactics and techniques. Gibbons wrote the Artillerist's Manual in 1860 which was published commercially by Van Nostrand. Although never officially adopted by the War Department, the manual was popular enough to call for a second edition in 1863.

The Civil War period engineer manuals were limited in number principally because of the technical nature of their contents. As West Point was the first engineering school in the nation, it was natural that many of the principal works in the field of military and civil engineering would be written or compiled by Academy graduates. Dennis Hart Mahan's famous course in civil engineering for the cadets was published in 1857 and his A Complete Treatise on Field Fortification, first published in 1836, was reissued commercially in 1861 and 1863.

Captain James C. Duane of the Class of 1848, West Point, produced a Manual For Engineer Troops which was so popular that it was printed in

---

[11]The board consisted of Captain William H. French, Class of 1837, West Point; Captain William F. Barry, Class of 1838, West Point and Captain Henry J. Hunt, Class of 1839, West Point. Hunt developed into one of the world's finest artillery generals during the Civil War.

three wartime editions, the last edition being the one published by Van Nostrand in 1864. Duane's writings were marked by a high degree of authenticity and professionalism. His Civil War combat service confirmed his qualifications as a manual writer. He was Chief Engineer of the Army of The Potomac from 1863 to 1865. In 1870, he wrote "Organization of Bridge Equipage of U.S. Army". In 1886, as a Brigadier General, he became Chief of Engineers.

Brigadier General James C. Duane, USA, (1824-1897). Chief of Engineers, United States Army (1886-1888). Author of A Manual for Engineer Troops: "Organization of Bridge Equipage of US Army."

*　　*　　*　　*　　*

The Civil War was noted for its large-scale initiation of numerous modern inventions and devices in warfare for the first time. Among these was the steam-powered railroad. The United States Military Railroad soon became one of the most vital adjuncts to successful campaigns in the field. Obviously, there was little military experience available in the areas of railroad operation, maintenance, and administration. Because of this paucity of experience, operational manuals were written as the war wore on. At first, the United States Military Railroads depended upon the operational patterns and policies employed by civilian railroad management. Herman Haupt, of the Class of 1835, West Point, was the first chief of the United States Military Railroads and, as a graduate who had resigned and entered railroading, he was a pioneer in establishing procedures for operating the railroads for the wartime army. His Military Bridges was published by Van Nostrand in 1864.

Captain George H. Mendell of the Class of 1852, West Point, served at the beginning of the war as Assistant Professor at the Military Academy. He later commanded an engineer battalion in the Virginia campaigns of 1863 and 1864, earning two brevets. In 1865, he wrote A Treatise on Military Surveying which was published by Van Nostrand. This was in reality a manual of surveying for essentially military purposes, that is, roads, fortifications, and emplacements.

Among the non-Academy producers of texts in the field of military engineering was George E. Head, whose System of Fortifications was published by Van Nostrand in New York. Another author of the same category was Thomas Kimber of King's College, London, whose work Vauban's First System, The Modern System, and Field-Works was published by Van Nostrand in 1852. This treatise, in three volumes, was in reality a translation and elaboration of the definitive works, by models of plaster which were colored with oil and mounted in strong frames, of Vauban, the famous French military engineer, designer, and builder of field fortifications. Kimber was far in advance of his time in the employment of scale-models as training aids for military instruction. In 1861, Kimber wrote Field Works; With Observations On Their Construction which was published in London by Longman, Green, Longman and Roberts. This was a practical manual on the construction of field fortifications.

The Signal Corps of the United States Army was developed primarily as the result of a young Assistant Surgeon's interest in the primitive signal system used by the American Indians he observed while serving on the frontier. During the Civil War, he established methods and means of visual communication over distances for purposes of military command and control. Throughout military history the need for a systematic method of communication on the battlefield has concerned commanders at every level. The advent of the electric telegraph answered this concern. However, there was a pressing requirement for a more simple and primitive device for communication than that of the telegraph key. The following extract explains that

> Lieutenant Albert James Meyers, a medical officer, is credited with adapting the Indian signalling system to the use of the army. While serving in New Mexico in 1854, he made a study of the Indians' methods of communication and from that devised the system of wigwagging with a signal flag. He presented his study to the War Department and in 1860 became the first Chief Signal Officer, with orders to create what was to become the Signal Corps. His methods were used by both the North and the South, and later adopted by armies abroad (Ref 27, p 177).

The Medical Department of the United States Army of the Civil War period was, like all other branches of the service, overwhelmed by the rapid expansion and reorganization for war. Consequently, medical texts and manuals were in scarce supply. The primitive state of the medical profession generally permitted the newly appointed military surgeons to continue their ministrations much as they had done in civil practice. However, the lethality of the weaponry and the severe nature of battlefield wounds caused much reference by American medical officers to the medical experience of the most recent war – the Crimean. In line with the experience of the other branches, the Medical Department found that it must depend upon private publishers for the furnishing of basic and advanced military medical texts and manuals. The principal purveyor of medical manuals was Lippincott of Philadelphia. This firm, as noted, also produced manuals for the other arms and branches but their "medical" line was most complete. The following texts and manuals published by Lippincott were "authorized and adopted by the Surgeon General, United

States Army, for use in Field and General Hospitals" according to information printed in the flyleaf of a Lippincott publication. The Hospital Steward's Manual was written by Joseph J. Woodward, M.D., Assistant Surgeon, USA and was intended to be

> ...A book of Instruction for Hospital Stewards, Ward-Masters and Attendants in their several duties. Prepared in strict accordance with existing regulations and the customs of the service in the armies of the United States of America, and rendered authoritative by Order of the Surgeon-General (Ref 25, see App C).

Gross's Military Surgery was written by S.D. Gross, M.D., Professor of Surgery in the Jefferson Medical College at Philadelphia. It was advertised as "A Manual of Military Surgery; or Hints on the Emergencies of Field, Camp, and Hospital Practice". Another important medical manual was Macleod's Surgery of the Crimean War. The prospectus of this volume read: "Notes on the Surgery of the War in the Crimea; with remarks on the Treatment of Gunshot wounds by George Macleod, M.D., F.R.C.S., Surgeon to the General Hospital before Sebastopol, Lecturer on Military Surgery in Anderson's University, Glasgow, etc. etc." William A. Hammond, M.D., Surgeon-General, USA wrote a treatise entitled Hammond's Military Hygiene which by 1864 had been published in a revised and enlarged second edition. Of considerable interest was the fact, that despite the primitive state of the medical art of Civil War days, an attempt was made to prescribe medical standards for Army recruits and, most importantly, for the detection of malingerers. Bartholow on Enlisting and Discharging Soldiers was advertised by Lippincott as "A Manual of Instructions for Enlisting and Discharging Soldiers, with special reference to the Medical Examination of Recruits, and the Detection of Disqualifying and Feigned Diseases by Robert Bartholow, A.M., M.D., Assistant Surgeon, USA". "Adopted by the Surgeon-General for issue to Army Medical Officers".

Other military-medical manuals were published by private firms. The medical-administrative paperwork problems were offered some type of solution by the advice, guidance, and methodology contained in Charles R. Greenleaf's A Manual for the Medical Officers of the United States Army, distributed by Lippincott in 1864. Of greatest significance was the volume, Notes on Nursing, written by Florence Nightingale and published by D. Appleton and Company, New York, 1861. This much-needed work was the product of the immortal nurse's experiences in the Crimea. The Hand-Book of Surgical Operations by Stephen Smith as published by Bailliere of New York in 1862 was advertised as "prepared for the military surgeon who previously had no small and convenient work suitable for a pocket companion..." (and who had to) either encumber himself with the large treatises... or rely upon his unaided memory...."

The Civil War exerted a profound influence upon every phase of the American military profession. This influence would cause changes to occur in tactics and techniques which have, in some instances, survived to the present day. The outpouring of written texts and manuals, official or otherwise, during the Civil War indicated the need for concise and understandable military knowledge. The Civil War produced combat experiences upon which to base novel and original tactical formations and techniques. The American military profession came of age in that struggle and it was no longer dependent upon the military theorists and practitioners of Europe for their translated and adopted versions of tactics. This was significant of a growing nation. The American people were becoming educated and literate in the art of waging war.

The United States Military Academy and its graduates must be noted as highly significant in the translation, origination, and authorship or editorship of the bulk of the military manuals and texts throughout our history. Thus, the flowering of military literature in America commenced during the period of 1861-1865. This great contribution to the training and doctrine of the American military profession, at all levels, served to establish a standard to which the amateur and civilian soldier could rally in time of war.

As was to be expected, the authoritative and professional tone of the small military academy on the Hudson was recorded and reflected in the writings of her sons. But not all the military thinkers and writers in the United States were graduates of the Military Academy. There were those officer non-graduates whose military training was secured either in the militia or in the hard school of war in the classroom of the battlefield. An outstanding example of non-Academy-inspired manual writing was in the area of the mounted service. From 1812 to 1833, the United States Regular Army did not possess a unit of cavalry. The militia of the several states carried on the mounted service traditions and training. Lieutenant Colonel Pierce Darrow of the Connecticut Militia and E. A. Jenks of Portland, Maine produced cavalry manuals for the mounted units of their respective militia organizations.

General Winfield Scott was not a graduate of the Military Academy. He was commissioned directly from civil law practice as a Captain of Light Artillery in 1808 - six years after the founding of West Point in 1802. His personal influence upon military literature from 1826 to 1865 was profound. While the bulk of Scott's "Manuals" or "Tactics" were essentially translations from the French or German, he, as president of several boards of officers, caused the foreign works under consideration to be adapted to American troops, terrain, and temperament.

Among the non-Regular Army writers of military Civil War literature was Captain Emeric Szbad whose Summary of the Art of War: Its Theory and Practice was published by Harper and Brothers of New York in 1863. Another writer in the field was Captain C. C. Andrews of the 3rd Minnesota Volunteers whose Hints to Company Officers was published by Van Nostrand of New York in 1863. Captain M. W. Berriman was the author of a manual entitled The Militiaman's Manual and Swordplay which was published by Lippincott of Philadelphia in 1861. Colonel Eugene LeGal of the 55th New York Infantry wrote School For Guides for the use of his regiment and the militia of the United States. This useful book was published by Van Nostrand of New York in 1862. Captain Egbert L. Viele of the famous 7th New York National Guard regiment wrote a Handbook for Active Service which was published by Van Nostrand in 1861. In the matter of regulations for the state forces there were several examples of specific regulations compiled or edited for state use. An Act For the Regulation of the Militia of The Commonwealth of Pennsylvania was approved in 1802 and published by Francis Bailey of Lancaster in the same year. Of considerable interest is the inclusion of a reprint of von Steuben's "Regulations" of 1779. Another example is General Regulations For the Military Forces of Ohio compiled by Henry B. Carrington and published by order of the General Assembly. This volume was printed by Richard Nevins, Columbus, Ohio, and distributed in 1861. Another specific work for the National Guard was the National Guard Manual by Colonel Stephen R. Pinckney of the 95th Regiment of the State of New York. This manual was published by Frank McElroy of New York in 1862 and 1864.

THE POST-CIVIL WAR PERIOD

After the signing of the surrender terms at Appomattox, the armies of the North and South were demobilized. The Confederate States of America ceased to exist and the Reconstruction period began. In the United States Army, Volunteers totalling 1,015,000 officers and men were disbanded and the military establishment shrunk in 1866 to 54,302 officers and men. This minimal size force was required to maintain law and order in the South and to contain the warring Indian tribes of the Great Plains area of the West. As far as the military profession in the United States is concerned, this period after the Civil War may be likened to the Dark Ages of European history (Ref 13, pp 298-353).

Emory Upton of the Class of May 1861 at West Point entered the Civil War immediately upon graduation and by his professional ability and courage rose to the rank of Brevet Major General of Volunteers within three years after his departure from the Military Academy. Upton's Civil War combat experience as a regimental commander and as a general officer stimulated his thinking along the lines of infantry tactical reform. His contact with non-regular troops, the Volunteers, prompted the writing of his monumental work, The Military Policy of The United States. But Upton's real concern was modernization of the obsolete infantry tactics he had witnessed on the bloody battlefields of the Civil War. He held to the thesis that infantry must possess a small, compact, self-sufficient maneuver unit if it would survive the fires of modern warfare. In 1867, Upton, as a permanent Lieutenant Colonel, issued his A New System Of Infantry Tactics Double and Single Rank Adapted To American Topography and Improved Fire-Arms. This little manual was as important to American military doctrine as von Steuben's "Blue Book" issued at Valley Forge almost a century before. Significant in defining a new tactical role for the Army it created the eight-man infantry squad to implement that role in combat.

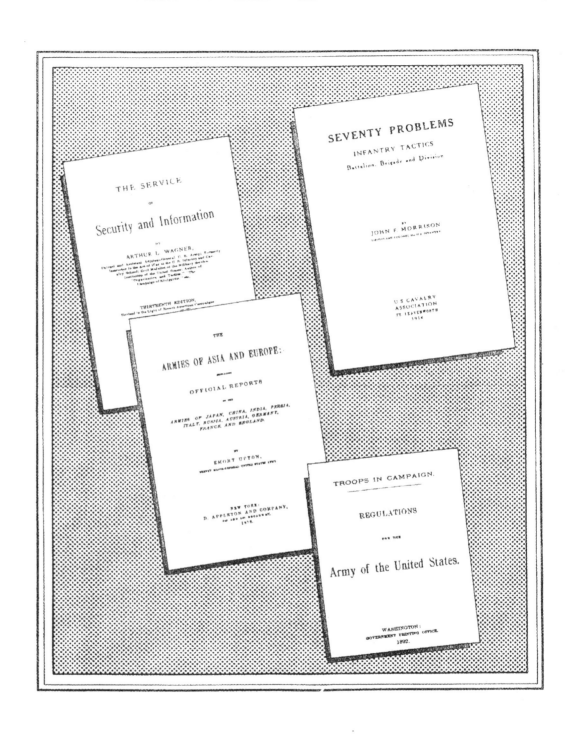

THE SERVICE
OF
Security and Information
BY
ARTHUR L. WAGNER,
[fine print illegible]
THIRTEENTH EDITION,
Revised in the Light of Recent American Campaigns

SEVENTY PROBLEMS
INFANTRY TACTICS
Battalion, Brigade and Division
BY
JOHN F. MORRISON
LIEUTENANT COLONEL 20TH INFANTRY
U S CAVALRY
ASSOCIATION
FT. LEAVENWORTH
1914

THE
ARMIES OF ASIA AND EUROPE:
EMBRACING
OFFICIAL REPORTS
ON THE
ARMIES OF JAPAN, CHINA, INDIA, PERSIA,
ITALY, RUSSIA, AUSTRIA, GERMANY,
FRANCE AND ENGLAND.
BY
EMORY UPTON,
BREVET MAJOR-GENERAL UNITED STATES ARMY
NEW YORK:
D. APPLETON AND COMPANY,
549 AND 551 BROADWAY.
1878.

TROOPS IN CAMPAIGN.

REGULATIONS
FOR THE
Army of the United States.
WASHINGTON:
GOVERNMENT PRINTING OFFICE.
1892.

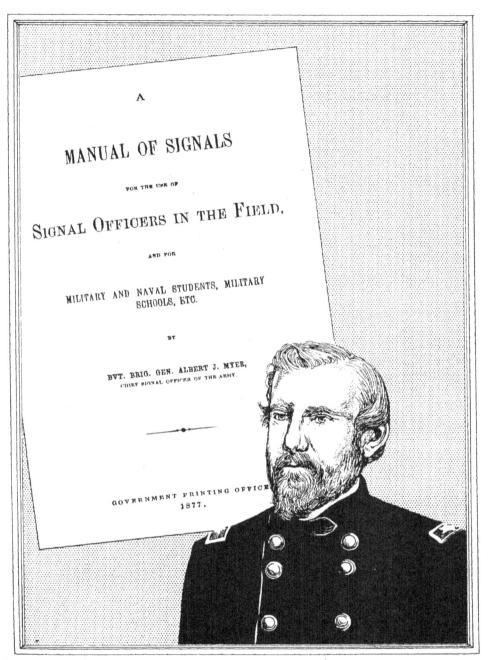

A

MANUAL OF SIGNALS

FOR THE USE OF

SIGNAL OFFICERS IN THE FIELD,

AND FOR

MILITARY AND NAVAL STUDENTS, MILITARY
SCHOOLS, ETC.

BY

BVT. BRIG. GEN. ALBERT J. MYER,
CHIEF SIGNAL OFFICER OF THE ARMY.

GOVERNMENT PRINTING OFFICE
1877.

Drawing from ' The Old Guard ' PIO Photograph

Published commercially in 1867 by D. Appleton and Company of New York, the new drill manual was soon what would be termed today "a best seller." With the approval of General U.S. Grant, Upton's new manual was adopted as "official" for the United States Army. Upton commented as follows in a letter to General Grant in explanation of the new system:

> ... The chief advantage claimed for the system is the adoption of a front of four men as a unit, the men of which, both front and rear rank, <u>preserve or maintain a constant relation to each other</u> (Ref 28, p 199; emphasis added).

Emory Upton's new drill manual was much more than just a drill regulation. In effect, it was a doctrinal field manual because of its exposition of combat performance through his advocacy of the use of extended order formations. Upton did not claim originality for all of his new manual. While some of it rested securely upon the Hardee and the Casey translations of pre-Civil War French manuals, he had shown creativity of the highest order. This creativity was evidenced by his adaption of the old tactics to <u>American terrain</u> and to battle conditions imposed by <u>improved firearms</u>, two conditions seldom adjusted to by earlier manual compilers and translators (Ref 29, pp 12 and 13).

Brevet Major General Emory Upton, USA (1839-1881). A Distinguished combat commander in the Civil War and brilliant writer of Upton's Tactics in which he devised the Infantry squad of eight soldiers. His Military Policy of The United States is the definitive work in the field.

*   *   *   *   *

Upton's new system adopted and employed by the infantry of the United States Army established the infantry squad as the smallest fire and maneuver unit in the service. His doctrine of extended order drill as a battle drill was, in many ways, ahead of its time. Upton's manual of tactics and drill was the regulation for the United States Army until 1891 when new drill regulations, incorporating changes in some instances, and improving upon his basic tactics, was published. Colonel William Ganoe in his definitive <u>History of The United States Army</u> comments that this year

...also marks the first issue by the War Department ment of three separate sets of drill regulations for "Infantry, Cavalry and Artillery." They represented the work of the best minds of the service in contra-distinction to the output of private publications (Ref 13, pp 366 and 367).

As noted above, the era marks a turning point in the use of privately published drill regulations and tactics by the professional soldier. While those published in the past often were granted the magic phrase "By Authority", others did not always possess the official imprimatur of the War Department. Sometimes, standardization of the drill and tactics was not achieved by the publishers. Theoretically, in time of peace centralization of production of all training literature was to be in the War Department and Government Printing Office. However, private publications were not frowned upon by the military customer - his only requirement was that they be in accord with the latest regulations and War Department policy. Indeed, it is in the period following 1891 that military literature began to proliferate as never before (see App D).

Colonel William Ganoe commented upon the Army School System of 1886 as follows:

> The schools in the army were by this time on a fair road to substantial advancement. It was little thought, when Lieutenant Arthur L. Wagner (Class of 1875, West Point) was sent to Leavenworth as instructor in military art, that he was going to be such a great factor in developing the curriculum of that school. For eleven years he was to influence its standards, he being there without intermission throughout that time. It was during this period that he wrote the Campaign of Koniggratz (1889), The Service of Security and Information (1893), and Organization and Tactics (1895). These works were particularly needed by the service. They suited the requirements of all branches and remained for years standard authorities on these important phases of military instruction. They were the result of wide research and able condensation and suited to the everyday use of troops. Ever since their issue the service at large has been influenced by them. It was through Wagner's efforts that the courses at Leavenworth were raised to a higher standard, especially in the field of military art (Ref 13, p 393; emphasis and parenthesis added).

Within the arms and branches of the service there followed a renewed desire for professional and technical instruction modeled after that offered at the General Service School at Fort Leavenworth. This movement toward branch training was highly significant as it required preparation of texts and manuals for resident instruction of the student officers and men assigned. In 1892, a "school of instruction" for cavalry and light artillery was established at Fort Riley, Kansas (Ref 13, p 364).

The death of General Emory Upton on March 15, 1881, under most tragic circumstances following an apparent mental breakdown induced by ill health, worry, and frustration, did not dim the luster of the works of this military thinker. His plan for professionalism in the officer corps of the United States Army survived. His Military Policy of the United States when finally published in 1904 by the government was hailed as a masterpiece of brilliant analysis of the continuing military problem confronting the United States. His Armies of Asia and Europe privately published at a considerable financial loss to Upton had sold less than 600 copies (Ref 30, p 121 and pp 155-159).

Colonel Arthur L. Wagner, USA (1853-1905). Distinguished author of textbooks and manuals on tactics. He is considered the "father" of the Leavenworth Schools, the present Command and General Staff College.

* * * * *

The writings of Wagner and others were to influence American military doctrine as it had never been influenced since the days of Mahan, Halleck, Casey, and Hardee. The service performed by these latter day military intellectuals was to cause them to function as originators, coordinators, and consolidators of American military thought. Borrowing from the campaigns and battles of the past, both European and American, these creative pioneers analysed military history for the lessons it contained. The study of the campaigns and battles of the great captains was deemed necessary by them to a thorough knowledge of the profession of the soldier.

In commenting upon one of the works on the art of war, published while he was on the Island of Saint Helena, Napoleon gave the following as the means of acquiring a knowledge of leadership:

> Read and reread the campaigns of Alexander, Hannibal, Gustavus Adolphus, Turenne, Eugene of Savoy, and Frederick the Great. Model yourself on them. This is the only means of becoming a great captain and of discovering the secrets of the art. Evolutions, the science

COMPANY COMMANDERS'
MANUAL
OF
ARMY REGULATIONS.

Being Paragraphs of the Army Regulations that Pertain to the Administration of a Company, Troop and Battery.   Compiled from the Regulations of 1901.

Compiled by
First Lieutenant William H. Waldron,
29th United States Infantry.

PRESS OF
HUDSON-KIMBERLY PUBLISHING CO.,
KANSAS CITY, MO.
1902.

of the engineer and of the artillerist may be learned
from treatises, as geometry is learned, but leadership can be acquired only by experience and by the
study of the wars of the great captains (Ref 31, p 274).

The relationship of the service schools to the military literature of
the period was definitely established by the interpolation of resident
instructional materials into existing and future Army Regulations and Drill
Regulations. As each school of each arm or branch was, in effect, the
fountainhead of professionalism for that arm or branch, its instructional
materials and instructors were basic to the writing of drill regulations or
doctrinal manuals. Technical manuals were produced by the various
schools such as The Engineer School and The Signal School. This
situation has obtained generally until the present time with exceptions.
Following Arthur L. Wagner at Leavenworth was a worthy successor,
Major (later Major General) John F. Morrison, Class of 1881, West Point.
Spaulding in his The United States Army In War and Peace had this to say
with reference to John F. Morrison:

This officer came to Leavenworth in 1906. Building
upon the foundations already laid, he developed both the
content and the methods of tactical instruction so that the
schools became definitely the intellectual center for the
Army.... But for a few years there was no uniformity of
thought or unity of doctrine. This the Leavenworth schools
brought about under Morrison, and his successors (Ref 15,
pp 397 and 398).

Early United States Army Regulations provided a modicum of
doctrinal guidance for commanders in the field and in garrison. But close
examination of these ancient volumes reveals that they were concerned
primarily with administrative and procedural matters pertaining to
command. Tactical dispositions and maneuvers were limited generally to
the establishment and conduct of outposts and advanced guard formations
and the layout of camps and winter quarters. The Revised U.S. Army
Regulations, 1863 conveys the following battle tactical guidance:

719. In attacking, the advanced guard endeavors to
capture the enemy's outposts, or cut them off from the
main body. Having done so, or driven them in, it
occupies, in advancing, all the points that can cover or
facilitate the march of the army, or secure its retreat,
such as bridges, defiles, woods and heights; it then
makes attacks, to occupy the enemy, without risking too
much, and to deceive them as to the march and projects
of the army.

728. In battles and military operations it is better
to assume the offensive, and put the enemy on the
defensive; but to be safe in doing so requires a larger
force than the enemy, or better troops, and favorable
ground. When obliged to act on the defensive, the advantage

of position and of making the attack may sometimes be
secured by forming in rear of the ground on which we
are to fight, and advancing at the moment of action. In
mountain warfare, the assailant has always the disad-
vantage; and even in offensive warfare in the open field,
it may frequently be very important, when the artillery
is well posted, and any advantage of ground may be
secured, to await the enemy and compel him to attack.

734. During the fight the officers and noncommissioned officers keep the men in ranks, and enforce
obedience if necessary. Soldiers must not be permitted
to leave the ranks to strip or rob the dead, - nor even
to assist the wounded unless by express permission,
which is only to be given after the action is decided. The
highest interest and most pressing duty is to win the
victory, by winning which only can a proper care of the
wounded be ensured. (Ref 26, pp 104-106).

In 1892, the United States Government Printing Office published a
small, pocket-size book entitled Troops in Campaign, Regulations For
The Army of the United States. This volume was a first attempt to write
combat doctrine in broad, general terms. An outgrowth of the work at
the service schools, the little book was the progenitor of the Field Service
Regulations, United States Army, first published in 1905 after an identi-
fiable General Staff had been established at the Headquarters of the Army
in Washington, D.C. There were new ideas indicated and items added to
the conduct of individuals in battle but, in general, the Regulations of 1863
was repeated. Paragraphs 264 and 265 were verbatim copies:

Article XV

BATTLES

264. Before the action, the generals indicate the
places where they will be; if they change position, they
will give notice of it, or leave a staff officer to show
where they have gone.

265. During the action, the officers and noncommissioned officers keep the men in ranks and enforce obedience if necessary. Soldiers must not be
permitted to leave the ranks to strip or rob the dead,
nor even to assist the wounded, except by express
permission, which is only to be given after the action
is decided. The highest interest and most pressing duty
is to win the victory, by winning which only can a proper
care of the wounded be insured (Ref 32, p 53).

The Field Service Regulations, United States Army, 1905, departed
radically from the products of the old "cut and paste" type Regulations.
There was strong evidence of the service school's influence in every
paragraph. New concepts and modern categorizations of combat and field

service were included. Of particular significance was the notice to be found on the title page: "Prepared by the General Staff, under the direction of the Chief of Staff, U. S. Army."

Troops in Campaign, as noted from the table of contents below, did not succeed in doing much more than consolidating ancient and traditional military customs and battlefield mores into a highly portable pocket-size handbook. There was little new in the thin volume but it was a step in the right direction - the creation of a true field manual whose contents, regardless of their obsolesence, were considered by higher authority essential to field operations in war. The contents of this first creditable attempt to give the field commander some doctrine are general and, sometimes, so vague as to be of little assistance. There appears to have been little theoretical base used. Its compilation seems to have depended not upon military history, as lessons learned and intelligently analysed, but upon conduct of the campaign as a series of logical and always re-curring events.

Article	Title
I	Organization of an Army in the Field
	Commands
	Artillery and Engineers
	The Administrative Services
	General Police
II	Tents, Baggage, and Baggage Trains
III	Headquarters, Depots, etc.
	Issue of Rations
IV	Intrenched Posts
	Camps
	Military Exercises
V	Reconnaissances
VI	Military Occupation, Contributions, and Requisitions
VII	Safeguards
VIII	Prisoners of War
	The Commissary-General of Prisoners
	Parole and Exchange of Prisoners
IX	Marches
X	Journal of Marches, Military Maps
	Specimen Pages of a Topographical Field Notebook
XI	Convoys and their Escorts
XII	Movement of Troops by Rail and Water
	Movements by Rail
	Movements by Water
	Transportation of Horses
XIII	Advance Guards and Outposts
XIV	Sieges
	Assaults
	Defense of Fortified Places
XV	Battles
	(Ref 32).

The Field Service Regulations, United States Army, 1905, was the product of the new General Staff and the combined intellects of the faculties of the service schools. Every page in this true field manual reflected the theoretical and professional approach to the problems of the field commander and troop leader. In place of glittering generalities, "Field Service Regulations" provided highly specific and detailed information for each combat situation expected to be met in the field. Creative and scholarly, this small manual approached the subject of combat operations in a realistic and intelligent manner. The volume, as published, must have satisfied the expressed desire of Major Gerlach in his cited letter to the Assistant Secretary of War, in 1902. The contents of a few pages are included below in order that the reader may note and compare the difference between "Field Service Regulations" and Troops in Campaign, its predecessor.

(e) Night marches
(f) Practice marches
(g) Crossing of bridges, fords, swamps, and frozen bodies of water
(h) Crossing of streams on ferries

Article VI. - Combat

General considerations
Fire
Advantages of the defensive
Advantages of the offensive
Summary
The attack of a position:
  The plan of attack. - The preparatory state. - The decisive action. - The pursuit. - Repulse.
The defense of a position:
  General principles. - The position. - The plan of defense. - Action in defense.
Night operations:
  General principles. - The different arms at night. - Preliminary arrangements. - The conduct of troops in a night attack.

Article VII. - Ammunition supply

For infantry
For artillery

Article VIII. - Subsistence

General principles
The field ration
The travel rations
The emergency ration
Modification of the ration and extra issues
Rations carried by a command
Methods of subsisting
Subsistence during movements of concentration
Fresh beef in the field
Fuel and forage
Issues

Article IX. - Transportation
(A) Wagon trains, ammunition columns, and supply columns:
  Wagon trains. - Ammunition columns. - Supply columns. - Reserve supply columns
(Ref 33).

The effect of the Spanish-American War upon the United States Army was profound. The collapse of the antiquated, obsolescent, and bureaucratic War Department at the beginning of that conflict constituted a national disgrace. The years of neglect of military affairs by both the public and the bureaucrats manifested itself in an ill-conceived and

haphazard mobilization. Indeed, without the loyalty, devotion, and professionalism of the small regular establishment and the dedicated citizen-
soldier - the National Guardsman - the war effort would have experienced
greater difficulty. As it was, the trials and tribulations of the hastily
assembled troops were serious enough to call for Congressional investigation
after the termination of hostilities (Ref 13, pp 371-375).

The professionalism of the 2,116 officers of the 25,000 strength Regular
Army, as noted above, was due largely to the improvement of the Army
school system. This school system, separate and distinct from the United
States Military Academy at West Point, consisted of The General Service
Schools located at Fort Leavenworth, Kansas. These schools were instrumental in instructing officers in the theory and practice of war. In so doing,
they required instructional materials pertaining to every phase of the military
art. From these instructional materials produced by the School instructors
evolved doctrine studies and textbooks. In these latter was the seed for the
field manual as we know it today.

In 1915, the Chief of Staff of the United States Army reported by Memorandum to The Secretary of War on the status of manuals and training literature, in general, throughout the service. Because of its historical significance the following extract is included below:

> As the Army has developed since the Spanish-American
> War, so has the number of government publications for
> the instruction of the Army increased. Prior to 1898 there
> were very few of these publications and in general consisted
> of the Army Regulations and the Drill Regulations of the
> several arms of the service. To these may be added the
> Manual of Guard Duty, which was first issued by an officer
> as a private publication in 1890, but in 1893 it was revised
> and printed at the Government Printing Office, and issued
> to the Army. Also Small Arms Firing Regulations were
> published as early as 1879, first in the form of orders and
> afterwards in pamphlet form (Ref 34; see App E).

Stimulated by the forward-looking, manual-writing military intellectuals
tactical reform was coming to the fore and proper attention was given by
service schools to this vital subject for the arms and services, or branches.
Military and tactical doctrines were developing slowly but certainly toward
concentrated and consolidated official compilations in the form of Field
Service Regulations and Drill Regulations for all the arms and technical
branches, such as the Signal Corps. In this period of our history of
military training literature in the United States Army, we approached
the critical point where a definite attempt was officially made to bring
tactics into consonance with weaponry. The effects of weaponry upon unit
formations and tactics were among the lessons derived from their studies
of military history by professional military educators and writers on
military subjects.

The need for concentration and consolidation of military doctrine and
policy for the guidance of the commander in the field was a problem common

to all armies. That certain of the world's military establishments recognized and attempted to solve this perplexing problem was noted by individual United States Army officers who had served abroad. Among those individuals was Major William Gerlach, United States Army-Retired, a veteran of the Civil War and Indian Campaigns, who in 1902 had written an article on the military forces of the United States. A non-Academy graduate, Major Gerlach entered the service as an enlisted man before the Civil War. In corresponding with the Assistant Secretary of War in a letter dated May 11, 1903, Major Gerlach queried:

> Will you permit me to make a suggestion here: We should have a thoroughly practical set of "Field Service Regulations," so as to insure uniformity for field work. I have given this matter much thought and I believe I am on firm ground. France, Austria, Russia, and Germany have good systems. The latter has, I believe, been translated into English and published in London.

> We are deficient in this direction; what we have is scattered in "Troops in Campaign," "Wagner" and "Tactics" etc., and not sufficiently thorough.

> ... The want always became apparent to me during our field work, and was more deeply impressed upon me when studying foreign regulations and still more during translation of a book on "Officers Field Service Education" (Ref 35).

Major Gerlach's trenchant remarks and pertinent recommendation to the War Department that doctrine and practice for field service be put into one volume between two covers came to eventual fruition. In effect, Major Gerlach had felt the need for centralized instruction and guidance for the officer in the field - a manual, or pocket handbook. Within two years, The United States Army Field Service Regulations of 1905 were published to the troops.

In the period after the advent of the "Field Service Regulations", there was evidenced a strong trend toward coordination and correlation of the Drill Regulations of all arms and services with the "Field Service Regulations". While this desire might be laid at the doors of the War College and the Service Schools and the newly formed General Staff, there were other cogent reasons. The primary one was the inspection of certain posts and military units of the regular army by inspectors from the War Department. The following extract from such a report, July 23, 1912, explains:

> It is earnestly recommended that the Field Service Regulations be brought up to date, and coordinated with the drill regulations of the different arms, especially with Infantry Drill Regulations, and that the manuals of the different staff departments be coordinated, not only

General Douglas MacArthur (1880-1964) as a young staff officer was instrumental in establishing the Field Service Regulations. As Superintendent of West Point, he instilled a high standard of training in its graduates. As Chief of Staff, he approved the development of the Field Manual. As Commander-in-Chief in the Pacific Theater in World War II, he saw training literature doctrine defeat a powerful enemy on land, sea, and in the air. In Korea, his Inchon Landing was a classic application of military doctrine.

with the Field Service Regulations but also with reference
to each other. The Field Service Regulations would be
more serviceable if properly indexed, as at present it is
frequently hard to find subjects desired, and much valuable time is wasted (Ref 36).

The above report was indorsed as follows:

...As this subject relates entirely to the work of the
General Staff, I recommend that if steps looking to the
desired end have not already been inaugurated, that the
advisability of referring the matter to the War College
Division be taken under consideration.

(s) Douglas MacArthur,
Captain, Corps of Engineers

On April 17, 1915, the Adjutant General of the Army indicated the
status of Regulations and Manuals in a Memorandum to the Chief of Staff.
In addition to his comments on the state of the literature of the military
art, the Adjutant General attached a copy of War Department Bulletin No. 3,
1915, which listed by title the Regulations and Manuals available (see App G).
A perusal of the list of official War Department publications available in
1915 indicates that private individuals and publishers were continuing to
be heavy contributors to the military knowledge of the military professional
and the citizen-soldier of the National Guard. Further notice is taken of
the fact that the works of the private authors and publishers usually centered
around military history, private translations of the memoirs and works of
foreign military authorities, and interpretation of individual analysis and
tactical principles. The War Department was continuing its unwritten and
ancient policy of encouraging the military intellectuals to publish. This
policy was to bear fruit in the war that was soon to follow.

In 1915, the Adjutant General of the United States Army reported to
the Chief of Staff that:

Since 1898 the number of publications has gradually
increased, until now there is a publication covering
about every line of work in the Army. At the time of
publication these several manuals were considered
necessary and desirable and it is believed that they have
been and will be of great benefit to the Army. Many of
these publications are intended for the use of specialists,
but in these times it is often necessary for an officer to
take up special work at short notice and these manuals
are then of great assistance. These manuals should be
complete and it is believed that any consolidation of them
for general use would tend to destroy the completeness
and convenience of them for use by specialists (Ref 34;
emphasis added).

In the years immediately preceding America's entry into World War I there was a flurry of military preparedness throughout the country. Of special significance was the Business Men's Training Camp which was conducted by the United States Army at Plattsburg Barracks, New York[12]: This indoctrination type, voluntary, military training was sponsored by the Military Training Camps Association, a patriotic group of substantial citizens who were concerned with the state of military unpreparedness of the United States. In 1914, because of hostile acts against the American Navy, the port city of Vera Cruz, Mexico, was occupied, first by landing parties and later, on April 28, by troops of the United States Army under the command of General Frederick Funston who had authority to demand an apology. By November the forces of General Funston were withdrawn without the apology as the offending government had collapsed (Ref 15, pp 403 and 404).

On March 8-9, 1916, the Mexican insurgent Pancho Villa crossed the border at Columbus, New Mexico, and attacked the garrison, which consisted of units of the 13th United States Cavalry. In a sharp fight, the invaders were repulsed but with American losses of 14 soldiers and 10 civilians, killed and wounded. A Punitive Expedition of 10,000 men commanded by Brigadier General John J. Pershing was organized and sent in pursuit across the border into Mexico. Intermittent skirmishing and scouting with and among the unfriendly Mexicans and troops of the Carranza government did not succeed in catching the elusive Villa. With diplomatic negotiations completed, the Expedition was withdrawn in January 1917. This partial mobilization of both Regular Army and National Guard units amounted to the following: there were in August 1916 a total of 48,000 officers and men of the Regular Army and 110,000 officers and men of the mobilized National Guard on duty along the 2000-mile border between the United States and Mexico. Elsewhere in the country there were 30,000 National Guardsmen on duty (Ref 15, pp 404 and 405).

The basic reason for the above review of the activities of the Army prior to World War I is to establish the foundation for the burgeoning interest in military training among the civil population. The greatest effect upon the public was to be noted in the mobilization of the National Guard units. Officers and men of the Guard were now on duty with their brothers, the Regulars, and they were desirous of performing their duties well and efficiently. This desire to excel meant individual study, which called for an inexhaustible supply of current manuals and regulations. The War Department could not furnish such numbers of volumes and the private publishers and military writers joined forces.

Few exclusively military publishers were in existence prior to World War I. These were generally offshoots of professional military associations

---

[12] In 1915 General Leonard Wood, commanding the Department of the East, organized instruction camps at Plattsburg, New York, for the voluntary training of civilians, which attracted public attention to the subject and accomplished much more good than their size would suggest.

such as The Infantry Association, The Cavalry Association, and professional journals, that is, The Coast Artillery Journal, The Military Engineer, and others. These organizations were semiofficial in nature and were considered authoritative and reliable by the professional and temporary wartime soldier and officer and the National Guardsman. One of the great strengths of the association-type publisher was his direct contact or connection with the active Army. This contact was often more than direct with Regular Army officers being detailed full time as members of the editorial and operating staff. Thus, the "Journal" cf a particular association became, in a sense, the mouthpiece or spokesman for the branch or arm of the Service represented. One of the most famed editors of this category was Colonel Joseph I. Greene, United States Infantry, Class of 1923, West Point, who served as Secretary of The Infantry Association and editor of The Infantry Journal from 1940 to 1959. His indirect influence as an editor and consultant upon the military literature of the World War II period was reflected in a high standard of effective military publication (Ref 20).

The American Army and Navy Journal, Incorporated, of New York, a privately-operated, magazine-type periodical was involved with publishing Colonel P. S. Bond's interpretive works on the drill regulations. As Colonel Bond's books were popular during World War I, the publisher continued to issue them and other military author's works after the end of the war. Among other civilian publishers was The National Service Company of Annapolis, Maryland and Washington, D. C., which was well known for its first publication of the Reserve Officers Training Corps Manual in 1920. The firm's successor was known as The Military Service Publishing Company and was a subsidiary of The Telegraph Press of Harrisburg, Pennsylvania. The leadership of the firm was vested in Edward J. Stackpole (now a Lt Gen, Pennsylvania National Guard, Retired) who was assisted by numerous expert military manual writers and editors employed privately from the active or retired list of the Army.

In addition to the firms noted previously for publication of a military "line" during the Civil War, there were newcomers to the field of military manual and textbooks publishing and sales. The most prominent was the George Banta Company of Menasha, Wisconsin. This company was engaged for many years in the field of academic and fraternity publication when suddenly it found itself in a new business. This business was the publishing of the "brain children" of Colonel James A. Moss of the United States Army. Colonel Moss of the Class of 1894, West Point, began his famous series of military textbooks and interpretations of Army regulations with the publication of his Officers' Manual in the early 1900's. By May 1917, the book had been published in six editions. His most famous work was the Manual of Military Training, which in the year before the declaration of war in April 1917, had sold over 40,000 copies. In his history of the George Banta Company, C. A. Peerenboom had this to say about Moss' best selling manual:

> Officer's Manual was followed by the Non-Commissioned Officers' Manual, the Private's Manual, and then

the Manual of Military Training. The last named was
the first book of its kind to be published in this country.
It combined a dozen or more subjects which had previously been dealt with separately by the Army organization itself. The Manual was especially adapted for use
as a text book covering the entire subject of military
training (Ref 37, pp 29 and 30).

Banta had been occupied with, in addition to Moss, other military
writers' publications some years before the 1917 period and company
records indicate the following early titles:

Moss,	Riot Duty	1911
Moss,	Private's Manual	1911
Moss,	Non-Commissioned Officer's Manual	1911
Sherrill,	Military Topography	1911
Holbrook,	Mess Sergeant's Handbook	1911
Hanna,	Tactical Principles and Problems	1912
Sherrill,	Military Map Reading	1912
Sherrill,	Rapid Reconnaissance	1912

In historical retrospect, the period from the American Revolution to
World War I might be termed the infancy and adolescence of the growth of
American military literature. In the beginning, the concept of military
instruction was borrowed from British sources with which the former
colonials were familiar. The foreign officers, in the persons of von
Steuben, LaFayette, De Kalb, Kosciusko, and others, brought fragments
of their military literature to the American Army. The foreigner who
influenced American military instruction and training to the greatest
degree was General von Steuben. His influence was established perma-
nently by his authorship of the first field manual for the troops of the
United States. His "Blue Book", as it was termed by the troops, established a basic concept - as to content and format - of what a field
manual should be. In essence, von Steuben held the belief that a manual
should contain information, doctrine, technique, and application based
upon doctrine and technique. His manual, Exercises For The Discipline
of Troops of The United States, followed that format literally.

In the post-revolutionary period there was little military literature
produced in the United States. Other than von Steuben's manual, which
survived until the 1830's, there were few military manuals available.
Those were generally of French, British, or German origin. There was
little or no motivation toward the creation of an American military
literature. This urge was not to come until the establishment of the United
States Military Academy at West Point, New York, in 1802. But it was not
to come into fruition until the few graduates had matured professionally as
army officers and intellectually as members of the Academy faculty.

One of the most interesting aspects of the development of American
military literature during the period was the important part played by
individual military writers, compilers, and translators. With the War

Department lagging in the production and revision of current and new manuals, the military intellectuals saved the day by publishing privately. Eventually, much of this outpouring of military theory and practice was absorbed into official manuals and other types of military publications. This situation was especially true in the matter of treatises written by members of the Military Academy faculty and the staffs of the service schools of the arms. The contribution of both these groups to the literature of the military profession was significant. It was especially so in view of the heavily weighted influence of European military literature upon the American scene. This foreign influence, for good or bad, was to dominate the field until after the end of the Civil War. The service school instructors' greatest service was their extrapolation of the lessons of military history into a usable and effective American military doctrine.

From the beginning, the basic method of the creation of manuals in the United States Army was generally centered around a Board of Officers. Usually, this Board was convened by direction of the President of the United States. The purpose of the Board was customarily stated in the convening order and, in the case of a manual, specific instructions were included as to the scope of the group's endeavors. Often the new manual, thus created, became known after the President of the Board, for example, the manual created by the Board of 1826, which was headed by General Winfield Scott, became "Scott's Tactics". The board technique of compiling or writing manuals was employed infrequently in the early days of the Army and only to draft a manual which was significantly new. In the final analysis, the professional stature of the personnel of the Board was highly significant of the ultimate end product. Hence, each board ideally contained the most knowledgeable officers in the Army. This was usually the case and it may be confirmed by notation of the eventual rank and command attained by the several board members. In essence, the manual produced by a Board of Officers could be expected to be a reflection of the professional standing of the individual members.

The American Civil War marked a tremendous advance in the field of military literature in the United States Army. By 1861, the Military Academy had graduated 1,966 cadets among whom were to be found the leading general officers of both Armies. The military intellectuals among this group had taken their profession seriously and limited numbers of them had written and published treatises, or translated and adapted foreign military manuals, for American use. A few contributed original works of value to the military profession. However, it should be noted that not all American military literature was produced by graduates of the Military Academy or members of the regular Army. Numerous officers of the various state militia, and of National Guard organizations contributed to the writing and compilation of manuals. For example, prior to 1833, the United States Army possessed no mounted units. Because of this situation much of the tactics and techniques for cavalry were developed and kept current by the State militia units.

The influence of Napoleon upon the tactics of the Civil War was overwhelming. This was especially so in the tactics of army units the size of a division, corps, or army. Essentially, this was because the mobilization and the commanding of units larger than a division had not been within prior American military experience. The masses of conscripts in the French armies commanded by the Emperor were duplicated by the combat requirements of the Civil War. The tactical dispositions on regimental and company levels were dated from Waterloo and they had not been modernized in accordance with the advances in infantry and artillery weapon lethality. Further, the manual of this period differentiated tactically, as to formations, not at all between the drill ground and the battlefield. Certain of the military thinkers, such as Emory Upton, as a combat unit commander, saw the need for different formations. In furtherance of his evaluation, he created the eight-man infantry squad and gave a new approach to dispersion, maneuver, and command in combat. But Upton's creative solution to the problem of the infantry mass on the battlefield was not to show itself in manual form until after the end of the war, in 1867.

The services of the private publishers in the field of military literature were highly significant in that they enabled public expression of private writings. Their aid in the times of peace, when the publication of military manuals by the government was limited, was a distinct and valuable contribution to the American citizen-soldier concept of national defense. In time of war, their contribution was noted for supplementing the limited publications of the Government Printing Office. Their devotion to this task enabled the soldier to possess an individual copy of the manual needed for the learning of his immediate duties. This fact contributed to the making of a better trained soldier and ultimately to a trained Army.

American military literature came into maturity during World War I when both governmental and private sources combined unofficially to furnish the base for training the millions of American citizens suddenly mobilized for service in combat. It was at this juncture that the years of patient and dedicated study and writings of the military professionals became invaluable and essential to the security of the nation. Their scholarly approach to the subject of war was instrumental in the melding of military theory and combat practice into usable and effective manuals. The period from von Steuben to Wagner must be considered historically as a pioneering era in which American military literature was advanced slowly but surely toward the goals of self-sufficiency and professional stature.

PART I

LITERATURE CITED

1. Sun Tzu, The Art of War (Trans. by Lionel Giles) Introduction by Brigadier General Thomas R. Philips, Harrisburg, Pa.: The Military Service Publishing Company, 1944.

2. Niccolo Machiavelli, The Prince, New York: The New American Library, 1952.

3. _____, The Art of War, n.p., n.d.

4. Cataneo, Most Briefe Tables, London: 1588.

5. Flavius Renatus Vegetius, The Military Institutions of The Romans, (Trans. by Lieutenant John Clark and edited by Brigadier Thomas R. Philips, USA), Harrisburg: The Military Service Publishing Company, 1944.

6. Colonel Oliver L. Spaulding, Pen and Sword in Greece and Rome, Princeton: Princeton University Press, 1937.

7. Virgil Ney, The Evolution of Military Unit Control 500 B.C. - 1965 A.D., Technical Operations Research, Combat Operations Research Group, Fort Belvoir, Virginia, CORG Memorandum CORG-M-217, 10 September 1965.

8. Major General Friedrich W. von Steuben, Regulations For The Order and Discipline of The Troops of The United States, Philadelphia: Printed by Charles Cist, MDCCC.

9. James Ripley Jacobs, The Beginning of the U.S. Army, Princeton: Princeton University Press, 1947.

10. Lieutenant W. E. Birkhimer, Historical Sketch of the Artillery, United States Army, Washington: James J. Chapman, Agent: 1884.

11. Lieutenant Colonel William Duane, Regulations To Be Received and Observed For The Discipline of Infantry in The Army of The United States, Philadelphia: Printed for the Author, 1814.

12. James H. Nesmith, The Soldier's Manual, Philadelphia: 1824. Republished by Riling and Lentz: Philadelphia, 1963.

13. Colonel William A. Ganoe, The History of The United States Army, New York: D. Appleton and Company, 1924.

14. "History of The Drill Regulations" by The Editor, Army and Navy Journal as included in Infantry Drill Regulations United States Army, New York: Army and Navy Journal, 1892.

15. Colonel Oliver L. Spaulding, The United States Army in War and Peace, New York: G.P. Putnam's Sons, 1937.

16. Colonel Samuel C. Vestal, "Frederick William von Steuben" Infantry Journal, July-August 1932, Vol. No. 4.

LITERATURE CITED (Continued)

17. Baron De Stuben, <u>Regulations For The Order and Discipline of</u>
<u>The Troops of The United States</u>, Albany: Printed and sold by Backus &
Whiting, 1897.

18. Brevet Major General Emory Upton, <u>Military Policy of The</u>
<u>United States</u>, Washington: Government Printing Office, 1917.

19. "History of West Point" <u>Catalogue, United States Military</u>
<u>Academy 1965-1966</u>, West Point: 1965.

20. <u>Register of Graduates and Former Cadets 1802-1963 of The</u>
<u>United States Military Academy</u>, Published by the West Point Alumni
Association, West Point: 1963.

21. Francis A. Lord, <u>They Fought For The Union</u>, Harrisburg:
The Stackpole Company, 1960.

22. <u>Battles and Leaders of The Civil War</u>, Vol. I, New York: The
Century Company, 1887.

23. General Francois V. A. de Chanal, <u>The American Army in The</u>
<u>War of The Secession</u>, Leavenworth, Kansas: G. A. Spooner, 1894.

24. <u>GPO Years, 1861-1961, A History of United States Public</u>
<u>Printing</u>, Washington: The Government Printing Office, 1961.

25. Colonel August V. Kautz, <u>The Company Clerk</u>, Philadelphia:
J. B. Lippincott, 1863.

26. <u>U.S. Army Regulations</u> (Revised), War Department, Washington:
Government Printing Office, 1863.

27. J. E. Whitman, <u>The Troopers</u>, New York: Hastings House
Publishers, 1962.

28. Peter Michie, <u>Life and Letters of Emory Upton</u>, New York: D.
Appleton and Company, 1885.

29. Virgil Ney, <u>Organization and Equipment of The Infantry Rifle</u>
<u>Squad: From Valley Forge to ROAD</u>, Technical Operations Research,
Combat Operations Research Group, Fort Belvoir, Virginia, CORG
Memorandum CORG-M-194. January 1965.

30. Stephen E. Ambrose, <u>Upton and the Army</u>, Baton Rouge:
Louisiana State University Press, 1964.

31. Colonel James A. Moss, <u>Officer's Manual</u>, Menasha: George
Banta Publishing Company, 1917.

32. <u>Troops in Campaign, Regulation For the Army of the United</u>
<u>States</u>, Washington: War Department, Government Printing Office, 1892.

33. <u>Field Service Regulation United States Army, 1905</u>, Washington:
The War Department, Government Printing Office, 1905.

LITERATURE CITED (Concluded)

34.   Memorandum of Chief of Staff, United States Army to Secretary of War, April 17, 1915 in Archives of the United States, Washington, D. C.

35.   Letter, Major William Gerlach to the Assistant Secretary of War, 11 May 1903, in Archives of the United States, Washington, D. C.

36.   Extract: Memorandum for the Chief of Staff, United States Army, July 23, 1912.

37.   C. A. Peerenboom, The George Banta Company Story, Menasha: The George Banta Company, 1965.

Secretary
ton, D.C.
ary of War,

tes Army,

Menasha:

PART II

WORLD WAR I

The period before World War I was marked by a minimal amount of
activity in the area of training literature. Revised Infantry Drill regulations
appeared with a degree of regularity, and individual officers of the regular
army and national guard produced treatises and "manuals" on various
military subjects. With the advent of The General Service School and The
School of The Line at Fort Leavenworth, faculty members of these institutions began to publish. Printed privately, or on the school press, as aids
to resident instruction, these publications supplemented and interpreted
the official regulations and doctrine. Written by military intellectuals,
such as Colonels Arthur L. Wagner and John F. Morrison, these studies
covered the areas of tactics and troop employment in battle. In this sense,
these essays were not manuals for the troops. In reality, they were theoretical and historical analyses of past campaigns and battle leadership. As
the products of some of the best military minds in the country they enjoyed
considerable prestige. They were of great value in the creation of a
professional approach on the part of the American officer to the subject of
war. The status of professional reading and study in the Army before
World War I is well told in the following extract:

> As for strategy in this "old" army, it was true
> that Moss' Officers' Manual, bible of the shavetail
> in the mid-1900's, listed suggested readings of the
> Great Captains and of past campaigns, and Wagner's
> Service of Security and Information was on many an
> officer's shelves. Upton's Military Policy of the
> United States, just rescued from the oblivion of dusty
> War Department files and published to the Army by
> Elihu Root, would be there, of course. The cavalry-
> man, too, probably had Carter's Horses, Saddles and
> Bridles. And the West Pointer, although memory of
> Dennis Hart Mahan was fading, had been indoctrinated
> by Fiebeger[13]. But in general it was not a studious
> officer corps; the club was so comfortable and the
> evenings so frequently taken up with post entertain-
> ment and visiting.
>
> Actually, the minimum requirements for an
> officer's professional reading in those days consisted
> of four volumes. These were the slim, blue-bound
> Army Regulations, with its incessant changes neatly

---

[13] Gustave J. Fiebeger (1858-1939), Class of 1879, West Point, Professor
of Civil and Military Engineering, USMA, 1892-1922. As such, he was the
successor to Dennis Hart Mahan. Further, he authored many military textbooks.

pasted into its pages; the Manual for Courts-Martial, Manual of Interior Guard Duty, and the short, fat, pocket-sized Drill Regulations of his arm or service, which contained all the answers (Ref 1, pp 29 and 30).

Historically, there is a great similarity of the pre-World War I period to the period before the American Civil War. At that time, the ante-bellum military thinkers of the schools of Dennis Hart Mahan and, later, Junius Brutus Wheeler of the West Point faculty had produced significantly important works. Henry Wager Halleck, William J. Hardee, Silas Casey, and Winfield Scott contributed studies, treatises, and drill manuals which were to be the text books for the battles of the Civil War.

Operating as an author of military textbooks since 1900, was James A. Moss, an infantry officer of the Regular Army. His first important work was his Officers' Manual. This volume was, in reality, a compilation of the customs of the service and an interpretation of the Army Regulations for the guidance of young and newly appointed officers, or graduated cadets. Published privately, the Moss manuals were highly popular before World War I and soon Major (later Colonel) Moss was busily engaged in preparing a series of training manuals which were to become bases of instruction of the United States citizen-soldier of that conflict. Moss was a most versatile and prolific author and compiler. The Officers' Manual was followed by the Noncommissioned Officer's Manual, the Private's Manual, and the famous Manual of Military Training.

Colonel James A. Moss, USA (1873-1941). Dean of the private writers of military texts and manuals. His contribution totalled over 37 books which were used as vital training materials in World War I.

*   *   *   *   *

A circular distributed by Banta for advertising purposes during World War I lists 63 different titles. Subjects other than those indicated above were included. These were Army paperwork, military aviation, flag signaling, trench warfare, machine guns, field artillery, etc. Of special value and significance to the World War I infantry officer and enlisted man was the definitive work by Captain Julian S. Hatcher, Lieutenant G. P. Wilhelm, and Lieutenant Harry J. Malony entitled Machine Guns. Published in 1917, this volume was a by-product of the

SELF-HELPS for the CITIZEN-SOLDIER
Being a Popular Explanation of Things Military
BY
CAPT. JAMES A. MOSS
AND
CAPT. MERCH B. STEWART
UNITED STATES ARMY
PRIVATES' MANUAL
(SECOND EDITION, REVISED AND ENLARGED)
BY CAPT. JAS. A. MOSS
United States Army
OFFICERS' MANUAL
COLONEL JAS. A. MOSS
United States Army
GEORGE BANTA PUBLISHING COMPANY,
MENASHA, WISCONSIN

experiments and training conducted by instructor-authors at the United States Army Machine Gun School at Harlingen, Texas (Ref 2, p 30).

The impact upon the Banta organization by the wartime demand for military manuals is indicated in the following extract:

> The declaration of war created a state of chaos in the Military Book Department almost overnight. There was not sufficient help nor room to care for affairs properly in the home office...It was at this time that R. E. Thickens first became a factor in Company affairs.. He...had been an officer in the National Guard for several years. He had recently returned from the Mexican border where troops had been mobilized to deal with the Villa revolution. He was first consulted... by George Banta, Jr., and asked to recommend someone... to head up the military book operations..R. E. Thickens offered to help out on a temporary basis...Between Thickens and George Banta, Jr. routine procedures were established...The demand for books rapidly outstripped the production capacity of the plant and both printing and binding orders had to be placed with outside sources... One of the printings of the Manual of Military Training... was run on an old Scott All-Size Rotary press...used regularly for printing soap wrappers...but it was legible and legibility was the only critical factor at the time (Ref 3, pp 30 and 31).

The Banta Company served the United States well and faithfully in the training of its citizen-soldiers for war service. Colonel James A. Moss, the professional military editor, made a distinct contribution to the eventual victory over the enemy. Hundreds of thousands of his books were used to train the hastily mobilized National Army troops of the United States. They served to supplement the limited, or often exhausted, supply of official government military publications. In this connection, it should be noted that Colonel Moss was most particular that his books conformed to the latest Army doctrine and regulations. The Moss Manuals, as they were termed, filled the gap efficiently and well (see App F).

Drill regulations and Field Service Regulations for infantry, cavalry, field artillery, and other branches were forthcoming from official sources at irregular intervals. Revision of drill regulations was infrequent, as the system was based upon Upton's Manual, published first in 1867. By April 1917, when the United States entered World War I, the latest revision of the Infantry Drill Regulations was dated 1911. Brought up-to-date in 1918, it survived as the guide for infantry. Provisional Infantry Drill Regulations, U.S. Army, Parts I and II, were first printed at Imprimerie E. Des Fosses in 1918 in France, and later published by the Government Printing Office, in 1919.

The United States Government Printing Office was a going concern by the time of World War I. When called upon to increase production because of the heavy printing requirements of the Armed Forces, the Public Printer found himself in a more favorable position than that of his counterpart of the Civil War period. Progress in the invention of high-speed printing machinery and the overall technical proficiency of the staff enabled the Government Printing Office to function under a greatly increased work load. The book, 100 GPO Years, describes the World War I situation. In view of the War:

> A greater part of the huge workload, in addition to the customary work for Congress and the various departments, was the military printing demand. The Army required millions of copies of drill books, handbooks, regulations, etc., clothbound, for immediate delivery. The Navy also needed vast quantities of printing and binding, with charges for these two departments totaling over $4\frac{1}{2}$ million (Ref 4, p 99).

In spite of the ability of the Government Printing Office to publish a huge amount of manuals, and other related military literature, there was still a dearth of personal copies of instructional materials for the newly raised National Army of millions of draftees. Historically, the pattern repeated itself in almost the same manner as occurred during the Civil War. Civilian printers and publishers jumped into the breach and filled the gap in the production of military training literature. Interestingly, many of the same firms which had published military volumes in the Civil War soon found themselves again in the military book business on a large scale. The historic desire of the American citizen-soldier to educate himself in the military art created an unheard of demand for military manuals and texts.

J. B. Lippincott of Philadelphia, D. Appleton of New York, G. P. Putnam's Sons and Harper Brothers of New York, and others revived their military publishing line.

During the period 1920 to 1930, the United States Army's Regulations and Training Regulations were published by the War Department in looseleaf binder format. The system was patently efficient and handy. Yet there were those individuals in the Army who believed that the system was awkward and too time consuming. The time-consuming feature centered in the amount of time required of the company or battery clerk to keep the binders current. In view of the constant outpouring of Changes and new Regulations, the average orderly room soon acquired a military counterpart of Dr. Eliot's famous Harvard Five-Foot Shelf of Books. Imposing and neat for the eyes of the inspecting officer, the heavy, metallic-bound volumes were considered the epitome of military efficiency. Woe be to the company commander whose file of these official tomes was found to be not posted up-to-date and not properly initialled by him.

There were further disadvantages to the binder system. Primarily, the Regulations, because of size and format, were not adaptable to being carried in the uniform pocket of the soldier for field use. Also, while they

r

I.

could be withdrawn easily from the loose-leaf file, they were difficult to retrieve. They were not compact, nor were they easy to handle, when bound, as the binders were bulky, heavy, and awkward. Eventually, every

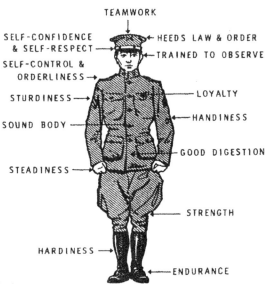

The Trained Soldier
(as noted by Col. James A. Moss)

conceivable subject for the government and training of the arms and services became an integral, but highly detachable, part of the system. The only Army Regulations to be found concentrated in one compact and easily handled volume were the Field Service Regulations and The Manual For Courts-Martial.

In 1930, Notes from the Chief of Infantry extracted from The Infantry Journal. Vol. XXXVI, No. 4, stated that the primary object of the Field Manual was

> ...to make available in condensed form for ready reference in the field the approved principles, doctrines, and methods that govern the training and employment of the various arms, together with such reference data and regulations as they need for mobilization, training, and field service. These manuals will be sufficiently comprehensive to be used as a basis for garrison and school training, supplemented when necessary by other authorized publications (Ref 5, p 418).

The basic field manuals were finally approved as the solution to the problem of the loose-leaf Training Regulations and the task of compilation begun by the various arms and services. But there was much more involved than mere compilation. Complete revision and doctrinal updating were to be accomplished at this time. This was an excellent opportunity to delete many of the old World War features still to be found in doctrinal areas and the Chiefs of the Army took full advantage of the situation to modernize their particular part of the Army. The following extract from the Infantry Journal of April 1930 is significant:

> The evolution of the field manuals has been a work of large magnitude. It has required careful planning, constant experiment, and close coordination. Although in its inception it was expected to be only a compilation of training regulations in convenient form, it actually has been a revision of the majority of the existing training regulations. The volumes concerning the arms and services were prepared by them and coordinated by a Board of Review in the office of the Assistant Chief of Staff, G-3, composed of representatives of the office of the Chiefs of Infantry, Cavalry, Field Artillery and Coast Artillery (Ref 5, pp 420 and 421).

The concept of the new Basic Field Manual was that it would concentrate all applicable information pertaining to a certain area of instruction, training, or doctrine into what today would be termed "a package" format, or treatment. This concept was particularly true of the Training Regulations for the Arms. The Technical Services publications were to be left generally as they were -- highly technical manuals for specialists. The Chief of Infantry noted that:

> In general, the Training Regulations which contain material as follows will not be replaced by the Field Manuals:
> (1) For purely peace-time training.
> (2) For mobilization, training, and field use which have for lack of space, been omitted in whole or in part from the Field Manuals
> (3) Of a special and not a general use, or not suitable or desirable in a Field Manual.
> As an illustration of the extent to which Field Manuals will replace Training Regulations, the Basic Field Manual, Volume II (Infantry Training Regulations), recently printed by the United States Infantry Association, will eventually eliminate twenty existing Training Regulations (Ref 5, pp 418 and 419; see App H).

In the post-World War I period, the schools of the arms were heavily involved in the development, or revision, of doctrine for their respective weapons and formations. At the Infantry School at Fort Benning, Georgia, during the 1929-1932 period, Lieutenant Colonel George C. Marshall, Virginia Military Institute, Class of 1901, served as the Assistant Commandant.

This was one of the most important episodes in American military history because his staff of "Marshall's Men" was composed of nearly all the future high-ranking general officers of World War II. Included among the future high commanders were: Omar N. Bradley, James L. Collins, Matthew B. Ridgway, George H. Decker, Joseph W. Stilwell, Charles L. Bolte, and others. The great strength of the Infantry School was its Tactical Department with military doctrine exemplified in the most practical way -- on the ground. When that was not possible, the map problem and tactical walk or ride, advocated and taught so long ago by Wagner and Morrison at Leavenworth, were brought into use. All students were required to research and to write and deliver, personally before a class of their fellow students, a military history monograph, which brought out the salient tactical points and principles of an historic battle. The following comment by Colonel Marshall about the influence of Colonel Morrison upon the students at Leavenworth, and upon him personally, and obviously upon American military doctrine, is a high tribute to this pioneer American military thinker:

> The students took to Morrison immediately: Marshall said. He spoke a language that was new to us and appealed very much to our common sense." The new language was in fact the language of thought applied to military problems in place of the traditional language of regulations." After listening to him it began to appear that the others were talking about technique and calling it tactics; that he talked the simplicities of tactics and cared (or maybe knew) nothing of technique...we (had been) given minute cuts on...errors in technique...for violating a fundamental tactical principle involved in meeting the situation. Simplicity and dispersion became fixed quantities in my mind, never to be forgotten. He spoke a tactical language I had never heard from any other officer. He was self educated, reading constantly and creating and solving problems for himself. He taught me all I have ever known of tactics (Ref 6, pp 98 and 99).

How tactical doctrine was arrived at and developed at the Infantry School (and at others) during the period of Lieutenant Colonel Marshall's service as Assistant Commandant may be illustrated in several ways. However, a significant example is noted from Marshall's relationship with Major (later General, and Chief of Staff) Omar N. Bradley, then recently made Chief of the Infantry School Weapons Section. Marshall mentioned in Forrest C. Pogues', George C. Marshall: Education of a General:

> ... that at the time there had been an obsession "with the idea of machine-gun barrages with the .30-caliber weapons, and (many veterans of World War I) wished practically to equip companies with a great deal of the communications set-up of a battery of artillery. I was opposed to this, not that I knew much about the details, but I was certain it was not a good thing to load down

an infantry company with so much equipment. I transferred Bradley to (head) of the Weapons Section and told him to take a close look at the machine-gun situation."
After careful study, Bradley's section gave a detailed demonstration of the problem. Marshall was delighted to find that the companies "already had enough equipment to do the whole thing," and that the presentation took half of the allotted time. He called it "the best demonstration I ever saw" and ordered that it be repeated for every class that came to Benning as an illustration of how to simplify instruction (Ref 6, pp 258 and 259).

With reference to a new infantry drill for the United States Army, Marshall was most instrumental in urging, like another military thinker named Upton, that the drill be made more applicable to the battlefield and less so to the parade ground. Traditionally, the basic source of the novel departure from the squad drill, which had served the United States Army for over fifty years, was French. Captain J. L. Collins (later Chief of Staff) was asked by Colonel Marshall to develop an improved drill based on that of the French Army, as noted by the Infantry Board at Fort Benning. But it was not adopted as regulation until after Marshall had become Deputy Chief of Staff in Washington. In addition to their instructional duties, the staff at Benning occupied themselves individually and collectively with the writing of new field manuals and the revision of the old ones. There was a considerable amount of experimentation with infantry tactics to complement new and advanced infantry weapons (Ref 6, pp 268 and 269).

General Marshall's tour at the Infantry School was marked by distinct advances in infantry tactics and techniques which were found later in the field manuals and training circulars prepared and published to the Army. It must be noted that at another service school, that is, at the Artillery School, there was a contemporary of George C. Marshall, Lesley J. McNair, who did for the artillery what Marshall was able to do for the Infantry[14] Marshall strove for one of the basic principles of war, simplicity, in his approach to the problem of doctrine and technique. He was progressive in his statement:

I insist that we must get down to the essentials, make clear the real difficulties, and expunge the bunk, and ponderosities; we must concentrate on registering in men's minds certain vital considerations instead of a mass of less important details. We must develop a technique and methods so simple and so brief that the citizen officer of good common sense can readily grasp the idea (Ref 6).

_____

[14] For many years General McNair was regarded as one of our country's leading artillery men. He served as assistant commandant of the Field Artillery School, and wrote a standard work on the tactical employment of the artillery battalion.

Marshall's approach to a combat doctrine of the combined arms was so realistic that he arranged for the faculties of the Infantry School and the Artillery School to exchange in order that infantry officers and artillery officers learn, at first hand, the doctrine of both arms. As Assistant Commandant, Lieutenant Colonel Marshall had direct responsibility for the operations of the various sections of the Infantry School under the command of Brigadier General Campbell King. One of the sections considered to be

General George C. Marshall, U.S.A. as Assistant Commandant of the Infantry School he encouraged the officers of the Faculty to develop simplified procedures... new manuals... and a new infantry drill... As Chief of Staff of the U.S. Army in World War II his leadership contributed to the excellence and effectiveness of training literature.

of prime importance to the dissemination of military doctrine and technique for resident and non-resident students, and the infantry at large, was History and Publications. The following extract from Pogue's George Marshall: Education of a General is significant of the future Chief of Staff's attitude towards the vital subject of training literature.

To the Fourth Section, in charge of history and publications, Marshall brought his old friend from China days, Major (later Major General) E. F. Harding. He contributed...the Mailing List, Harding developed into a significant professional aid by publishing tactical problems to be solved by readers. Marshall, in summarizing the state of training at Benning just before he left, singled out the Mailing List. "It now has readers", he wrote, where formerly it only had subscribers. Its small problems make the real picture of a battle. It is being used throughout the country by National Guard and reservists, and not filed or dumped in the waste basket:...Harding's section; prepared Infantry in Battle (Ref 6, p 259).

WORLD WAR II

The preparation and revision of training literature was a continuous task. The complexity of equipment used in modern war and the great number of different type troop units made the initial program of training literature tremendous. When our experiences in training or in combat uncovered faults or indicated improvements training guides were promptly revised or amended. Army Ground Forces Report, World War II.

The United States Army entered World War II with a solid tradition of training literature and materials developed by the Regular Army during the period of peace from 1918 to 1941. This material was to be of great value at the beginning of the mobilization for World War II, but a large amount of it was either obsolete, or not well suited for consumption of the citizen-soldiers who were called to the colors by the millions. Written by military professionals for the small peacetime Regular Army, National Guard, and Reserve Corps units, it required updating, revision, and vitalization for it to be interesting and understandable to the wartime soldier. The following trenchant observation, noted in an Army Ground Forces Report, is quoted in support of the above observation:

Pre-Pearl Harbor training literature, written generally in a somewhat stilted, military style, had been largely uninteresting or incomprehensible to the new citizen army. In addition, owing to peacetime economy measures, illustrations had been few. Army Ground Forces instituted a new style of field manual writing - aimed particularly at the expanding army of recent civilians - and began to use illustrations, photographs, and drawings as profusely as possible to leaven the text.

Gradually, most of the non-War Department publications which had come into use at the beginning of the war were suspended, and steadily-increasing distribution was made of authentic doctrine. Two or more former manuals were frequently combined into one better document. Large quantity production of some urgently needed manuals was accomplished at Army Ground Forces field printing plants (Ref 7, p 18).

The pressure exerted upon the Government Printing Office during World War II was considered by the Public Printer to have been the greatest in its history. The demands of wartime printing were almost as pressing as the prosecution of the war itself. The importance of military training literature is well expressed in the following extract from 100 GPO Years 1861-1961:

> ...the story of Government printing during World War II was one of continuing and serious drama, for never in its history had the Office been faced with such heavy military and civilian printing demands.

> The soldier and sailor may fight a war and push the enemy back on all fronts - by air, by water, by land; the manufacturer and farmer may produce essential tools and sustenance; the civilian branch of the Government may maintain controls on the home front - all highly essential; but without the printer and his constant flow of printed technical manuals, orders, regulations, etc., neither the soldier, the sailor, nor the others could carry on in this technical age (Ref 4, p 131).

In World War I, the Government Printing Office found itself faced with the problems of printing production on an unprecedented scale. In World War II, the problem was the same except for the volume and types of manuals required. With the complex development of the military art since World War I, there were many more requirements than just that of infantry and other drill manuals. New dimensions had added newer tools to the trade of war and these tools had to be explained with care and accuracy to the millions of citizen-soldiers whose basic task was their operation in combat. This trend is shown significantly in the following:

> The heads of U.S. fighting forces stated that with the unprecedented influx of new personnel, ships could not sail until manuals describing their gear and equipment were printed and delivered, plane pilots would be grounded without vitally needed printing, and bombs could not be dropped unless certain printed jobs were produced to show the bombardier how and where. Every gun, every tank, and every piece of ordnance equipment required printing for its manufacture, operation and maintenance (Ref 4, p. 132).

In addition to the major problem of scheduling military printing there were additional and perplexing problems of storage and distribution. The publication of a manual was significant but the manual was of little value unless it could be placed swiftly and surely in the hands of the service men who required it. The establishment of warehouses, on a regional basis, near the large military training centers in the continental United States helped to solve the storage problem and facilitated distribution. Another solution to the priority of distribution was achieved by calling on the commercial printers, as in all previous national emergencies. How this was done is best explained in the extract below taken from 100 GPO Years 1861-1961:

> Printing for the War Department presented the same difficulties (scheduling) as Navy work. The volume was prodigious and production schedules were almost impossible. By the end of May 1943, War Department printing alone was 50% greater than for the entire Government in peacetime, delivery requests were completely unrealistic. The GPO was fully aware of the vital need for printing in the prosecution of the war. But it knew no magic formula that would place printed matter in War Department warehouses the day it was ordered...

> A working basis was finally reached. To insure delivery according to schedule, emergency jobs were to be produced in the Office. Standard manuals (largely reprints) were to be produced commercially. Suitable paper was stored in the warehouses. The GPO furnished printing media (tenaplate molds, shell, and patterns for printing plates, reproduction proofs, etc.,) direct to the participating printers, and production continued simultaneously all over the country. All follow up was the responsibility of the War Department and resulted in marked improvement in deliveries (Ref 4, p 142).

The extensive wartime requirement for the printing of military publications had its effect upon the national stockpile of printing paper. The domestic paper pulp mills could not possibly supply the need and foreign sources of paper, such as Norway, were utilized. Paper stock supply was limited in World War II just as it had been in the Civil War and in World War I. The Government Printing Office enjoyed no special ration or allotment of paper stock. Throughout the period of World War II, the Government Printing Office competed for paper with private commercial printers and the other Government departments. During the war years, the Government Printing Office used a total of 27,000 freight car loads of paper stock which added up to 1,350 millions pounds of paper. With the emphasis on military publication production it must be assumed that the bulk of this huge total went into manuals and other essential military literature. Statistically, the Government paper requirement demanded 60 percent of domestic mill capacity on certain grades and types. The overall paper requirement of the Government was about 40 percent of the national output (Ref 4, p 140).

The procurement of privately printed technical manuals became highly important to the overall war effort. This was so, primarily, because of the urgency of the need for the training documents concerned. How this huge block of military training literature was produced through the cooperation of private industry is explained in the extract below:

> One of the most important procurement jobs was the buying of War Department technical manuals. Schedules provided for printing these publications in 21 days and were approved only after the Public Printer had engaged in lengthy negotiations with contractors.... The work was rotated among five contractors in New York, and the program was instrumental in securing urgently needed wartime publications on a regular schedule.... On many occasions, it was necessary to reduce the normal 21 days allowed for production. U.S. troops crossed the Rhine at Remagen over a bridge which was assembled from specifications and instructions printed in a manual produced in 10 days (Ref 4, p 136).

The direct connection between battle and the drill book, or field manual, has been shown throughout this study. To a marked degree, the technical manual mentioned above exemplified the value of the printed work in the technical aspects of combat.

The cited history of the Government Printing Office does not mention the non-contract, commercial, production of military literature during the periods covered. As noted, civilian publishers of military literature have contributed, in no small measure, to the dissemination of military knowledge during all of the national emergencies beginning with the Civil War. The majority of these publishers operated privately and commercially with no connection with the Government Printing Office. There were exceptions, those who were granted the phrase "By Authority of the War Department" to print and sell "official" Government publications. As late as World War II, the U.S. Infantry Association and others were granted similar permission.

The Military Service Publishing Company of Harrisburg, Pennsylvania became the principal civilian, commercial, publisher of military texts and manuals during World War II. The publishing house fell into this position naturally by virtue of long and constructive association, since post-World War I days, with the National Guard and the Organized Reserve of the United States Army. The peacetime publications of the company were well and favorably known to the hundreds of thousands of citizen-soldiers called to service with the colors. The George Banta Company of Menasha, Wisconsin, famous for the Moss Manuals of World War I, did not become deeply involved with military manual publication - except for the publication of the renowned Bluejacket's Manual of the U.S. Navy for the United States Naval Institute at Annapolis, Maryland. The passing of Colonel James A. Moss, in an accident during the early part of the war, left a gap in the ranks of the military authors and writers that was never filled. Operational control of the writing and revision of official military literature was securely retained by the United States Army. Hence, individual military writers and interpreters of regulations and manuals did not appear in large numbers. The names of well-known military writers of earlier days, such as Colonel P. S. Bond, appeared in print as either author or publisher of interpretative works on Infantry Drill Regulations. However, during the World War II period, no one individual military author was especially significant or prominent in the United States.

With the deactivation in 1942 of General Headquarters, and the activation of Headquarters, Army Ground Forces under the command of Major General (later Lieutenant General) Lesley J. McNair, training for combat was soon operating on the plan devised by General McNair and his highly professional training staff. Army Ground Forces was occupied with many important missions and the keen and incisive mind of General McNair served as a balance wheel to insure that the Ground Forces were properly organized and trained for modern combat. Among the major missions of Army Ground Forces was supervision of the concept, initiation, and production of Field Manuals for the arms and services within its purview (see App I).

In his Report On The Army, made during the period July 1, 1939 to June 30, 1943, General George C. Marshall, Chief of Staff, commented:

> The vital importance of adequate training in the technical warfare of today is evident. Such training involves not only the basic elements of military science, but their coordination into teamwork involving the platoon, company, battalion and regiment, and later, combined training of the various arms into divisions and army corps capable of a sustained and coordinated effort on the battlefield. The organization of training centers, expansion of our school system, the activation of new units, the development of new training doctrines, and the conduct of maneuvers, have been the primary responsibility of the Army Ground Forces which, under the command of Lieutenant General Lesley J. McNair, has achieved remarkable results that today are paying heavy dividends on the battlefield (Ref 8, p 95; emphasis added).

Tactical doctrine for World War II was found, initially, in the then existing Field Service Regulations which had been revised periodically since their inception in the early 1900's. But this was a different kind of war than America had ever faced. The employment of air power and armor was to call for new and strange doctrinal approaches to the conduct of war in the air and on the ground. In addition, the war was a global one and the terrain varied from the deserts of Africa to the mountains of Italy and the jungles of the Pacific Islands. Hence, tactical doctrine had to keep pace with the combat as it developed. How this was done is explained below:

> While American military doctrine was sound at the beginning of the war, it was necessary that it be kept constantly up-to-date. This was accomplished by

maintaining a group of observers in every theater. They
furnished written reports and returned to this country
periodically to make personal reports to specific operating
agencies. Frequently they visited the training schools to
bring a breath of combat to domestic soldiers. As the
war continued a limited number of combat-experienced
officers were brought back to occupy positions on the
staff of Army Ground Forces and its subordinated elements.
Some were assigned to the teaching staffs of the various
service schools to pass on their combat know-how to troops
in training (Ref 7, p 18).

General Lesley J. McNair, USA (1883-1944). As Chief of the
Army Ground Forces, during World War II, he was directly
responsible for the quality and effectiveness of the manuals
concerned with their training. As a professional artillerist,
he was author of a basic training text which was used at the
Artillery School at Fort Sill, Oklahoma.

In World War II, the United States
Army consisted of two major forces -
the Army Ground Forces and the
Army Air Forces. For the second
time in its long history, the Army
was to fight a war in which air, as
well as ground, action occurred.
The problem of close combat support
of the ground forces by air units
became one of the most difficult for
the respective commanders to resolve.
In essence, the principal problem
centered around the question of who
commanded the air units when they
were in direct support of the ground
forces. This was an area in which
the Germans had excelled in Africa
and other combat zones. There was
a need for an American doctrine.
There was dire need for written
guidance for both ground and air
element commanders. In essence:

*   *   *   *   *

The principles of centralization and decentralization
of air support strength were in conflict. Centralization
would require the attachment of air forces to the highest
Army commands, allotting these forces only temporarily
to lower units as occasion required. This method pre-
served the fluidity and mobility of support aviation and
made possible the assembling of mass striking power
against the most important objectives. This was the
principle urged by General McNair for the organization

of tank destroyer units. Decentralization, through attachment of air support to lower commands, would speed up the local delivery of support. The bad feature of decentralization was to immobilize air strength in places where it might not be needed or to fritter it away on local and insignificant missions. The bad feature of centralization was to set up long command and liaison channels and to slow down the process of getting air assistance to ground troops (Ref 9, p 63).

FM 31-35, Aviation in Support of Ground Forces, was written by Colonel Wm. E. Lynd and other staff officers of General Headquarters prior to the activation of Army Ground Forces. Based upon study of the various reports on Air-Ground operations in the Army maneuvers conducted from November 1940 to January 1941, the draft field manual was submitted to the War Department on 31 January 1942 for approval. How the new doctrine was promulgated through the medium of the manual is shown in the extract below:

> On air-ground command relations the doctrine was flexible. "An Air Support Command," said the manual, "is habitually attached to or supports an army in the theater." Normally the air support commander was to function under the army, theater, or task force commander. He would allocate, and in exceptional cases might attach, aviation units to subordinate ground units, but it was emphasized that the air support commander was to control all participating aviation. In general, the principle adopted was that of centralization (Ref 9, p 64).

This example of how new doctrine was disseminated to the Army, after careful study of maneuver and combat reports, is significant of the development of doctrine during an active combat period. At the service schools, such as the Infantry School at Fort Benning, FM 31-35 was supplemented by the writing and printing of Air-Ground Training Bulletins. These interpolative documents were issued to all infantry course students and to all units of the infantry divisions of the Army. Dr. Kent Roberts Greenfield, formerly Chief Army Historian during World War II, noted as follows:

> Having failed to get independence, the Army Air Forces leaders got their doctrine of command recognized by the War Department in one of its Field Manuals, No. 31-35, issued in April, 1942 (Ref 10, p 102).

As the war in the air and on the ground progressed there was marked improvement in the tactical coordination of air and ground forces. Further definition and clarification of doctrine for the Army Air Forces was to be found in FM 100-20, Command and Employment of Air Power, issued by the War Department on July 21, 1943 (Ref 10, p 107).

The changes in tactical doctrine were included in the field manuals in preparation, or revision, at the various service schools of the arms.

Technical manuals describing the care and employment of equipment and materiel were prepared for the use of the troops in training and in the field. New equipment called for printed operational instructions and these were produced usually by the school or agency sponsoring the item. Thus at the beginning of World War II, a sharp line of demarcation was drawn between the field manual and the technical manual. How the War Department approached the complex problem of keeping the troops up-to-date tactically and technically is shown in the extract below:

> With the adoption of Selective Service and induction of the National Guard, GHQ faced the problem of turning most of the able-bodied male population of the country into soldiers. Existing field service regulations provided the tactical doctrine to which the new men were to be introduced. Technical manuals described the care and employment of equipment. On 9 August 1940 the War Department initiated a series of training circulars, which were to keep the Army abreast of current developments pending the publication of new or re-edited training and technical manuals. Training Circular No. 2, dated 19 September 1940, briefly outlined the instruction to be given to inducted men. Mobilization Training Programs (MTP's) specified in more detail the thirteen-week basic training to be given in various branches of the service (Ref 9, p 17).

In the Army, prior to the outbreak of World War II, training literature, that is, field manuals, field service regulations, and technical manuals were generally produced and revised by the service schools of the arms. Field service regulations were kept current by the Staff School and the War College. On the operating levels, the field manuals were usually within the purview of the service school or chief of the arm concerned, that is, The Infantry School, The Artillery School, The Engineer School, The Chief of Infantry, The Chief of Cavalry, etc.

For example, at the United States Infantry School at Fort Benning, Georgia, and at other Service Schools of the Arms, before Pearl Harbor, training literature containing both doctrine and technique was produced in various formats. With reference to the Infantry School there was the Mailing List so highly thought of by General Marshall. This extra-curricular training effort consisted primarily of professional articles and tactical problems written anonymously by Staff and Faculty members in their spare time and with no honorarium given or expected. Individual Army infantry officers subscribed, at their own expense, to the Mailing List in order to secure the latest instructional and tactical trends. At the Infantry School and the schools of the other arms, current Infantry Drill Regulations and Field Manuals were under constant revision supervised by the Training Literature and Visual Aids Section. The Tactical Committee and Weapons Committee of the Infantry School were charged with revision of Field Manuals covering these particular subjects. Editing and format were under the direction of Training Literature and Visual Aids Section of

The Infantry School. The approving authority between the Infantry School and the War Department was, at this point, The Chief of Infantry in Washington. After Pearl Harbor, the Infantry School became the center for infantry training of the entire Army. Literally, officer candidate schools were established overnight. In addition, thousands of officers and men were ordered to Fort Benning to pursue formal courses in the basic and advanced tactics and techniques of infantry combat.

The cry was for printed training literature, Field Manuals, Training Bulletins, Mobilization Training Programs, and changes to current training materials. Anything with which to train! At this juncture in the history of the Infantry Field Manuals, during World War II, there was a highly qualified infantry officer in charge of Training Literature at the Infantry School, Lieutenant Colonel (later Brigadier General) Sterling A. Wood of the Class of 1917 at West Point who gave the training literature effort professional guidance, leadership, and dynamic direction [15] Scanning each incoming and outgoing class for writers, editors, and artists, Colonel Wood enlarged his staff to do the job and do it effectively. Working behind screens in Room 342 on the third floor of the Infantry School, these people under Colonel Wood's direction created, wrote, revised, and illustrated the infantry field manuals for the infantry of World War II.

As the war developed overseas, the writers of field manuals at the various service schools were faced with the problem of updating combat doctrine. Army Ground Forces solved this situation by maintaining Ground Forces Boards in the different theaters. These boards were staffed with observers who accompanied units into combat and brought out suggestions, new ideas, and comments upon weapons, tactics, and doctrine. Eventually, this vital information reached the service schools and training centers concerned to be incorporated in doctrine, revised field manuals, and modernized and revised training schedules. Service schools, such as the Infantry School, sent faculty members overseas with the mission of observing current combat operations with a view toward incorporation of tactical changes and weapon techniques into the school's curriculum. With reference to American military doctrine, to be later reflected in the manuals and training literature, the following comment is noted:

> Evaluation of lessons learned from current operations abroad and numerous changes in our organization and equipment have necessitated a wide revision of training literature for the Army. Sixty field manuals and one hundred sixty technical manuals were prepared and printed during the fiscal years (Ref 8, pp 27 and 28).

Throughout the Army during World War II there was a concerted effort made by all concerned to make instruction more vital, meaningful, and effective. The point of departure was essentially the basic source of all

---

[15] Author of Riot Control, Harrisburg, Pa.: Military Service Publishing Company, 1941.

CPSIA information can be obtained at www.ICGtesting.com
Printed in the USA
BVOW08s1205081014

370011BV00021B/778/P